The Book Of The Daffodil

S. Eugene Bourne

THE BOOK OF THE
DAFFODIL

BY THE

REV. S. EUGENE BOURNE, B.A.

TRINITY COLLEGE, DUBLIN; VICAR OF DUNSTON BY
LINCOLN; FELLOW, AND MEMBER OF THE NARCISSUS
COMMITTEE, OF THE ROYAL HORTICULTURAL SOCIETY

"He that has two cakes of bread, let him sell one
of them for some flowers of the Narcissus, for bread
is food for the body, but Narcissus is food of the soul."

MOHAMMED.

JOHN LANE: THE BODLEY HEAD
LONDON AND NEW YORK. MCMIII

Turnbull & Spears, Printers, Edinburgh

Printing Statement:

Due to the very old age and scarcity of this book, many of the pages may be hard to read due to the blurring of the original text, possible missing pages, missing text, dark backgrounds and other issues beyond our control.

Because this is such an important and rare work, we believe it is best to reproduce this book regardless of its original condition.

Thank you for your understanding.

MAGNI-CORONATI
(A Johnstoni form)
NARCISSUS "CECIL RHODES"

A DEDICATION

To Him who formed the flower my heart I raise,
Whose Name is "Wonderful," His tribute praise,—
To Him Who subjected His work to man,
Enabling one, whose life is but a span,
To bring such possibilities to light,
Such new sweet beauties to the ravished sight,—
Who first a flower and then a man could make,
Then give man skill of simple flowers to take
And with laborious pains and patient care
Call forth a multitude of forms so fair:—
They lift my thoughts from earth to heaven above,
I own His Wisdom and I trust His Love.

S. Eugene Bourne.

TO MISTRESS DAFFODIL

WILL they laugh at your old-fashioned gown,
   Daffodil?
At your simple and quaint little gown,
As you enter the streets of the town;
Pass you by with a sneer and a frown,
   Daffodil?

  .   .   .   .   .

Nay tell them old fashions are best,
   Daffodil.
Old friends are the dearest and best,
And the flower we would wear at our breast
Is the one longer loved than the rest,
   Daffodil.
     MARGARET JOHNSON (*see Preface*).

PREFACE

This little book is intended to supply a want, such as I felt keenly myself some fifteen years ago when beginning to grow Daffodils in "deadly earnest." Had some such guide been then at hand, I should have been saved considerable expenditure of time, money, and misdirected energy.

There is here set down the result of my own personal experience gained in cultivating a large and representative collection of over 200 varieties during many years, also in exhibiting, and of late years judging Daffodils; with the addition of sundry useful facts and opinions, which I have noted from time to time from various sources. The book has grown out of a Paper on the "Cultivation of the Narcissus in Gardens" read before the Royal Horticultural Society in the year 1900 (*Journal of R.H.S.* Vol. xxv. p. 39). Most of the advice then given is now repeated and brought up to date, but only forms a small part of the whole; it has been largely supplemented by other matters of Daffodil lore, and it is hoped that the information now gathered together in a handy volume may help the lover of Daffodils, not only to grow good flowers, but also to maintain his collection at a high standard, and generally to hold his own with other Daffodil people.

I beg to acknowledge thankfully the assistance I have received from—

Mr J. G. Baker's "Amaryllideæ."
Mr F. W. Burbidge's "The Narcissus."
Mr Barr's little book "Ye Narcissus."

Mr Robinson's "English Flower Garden"; and last but not least the invaluable Journals of the R.H.S. I wish also to express my thanks to the publishers of *The Country*, for their permission to reprint my article on "Exhibiting Daffodils," which with some few alterations forms chapter xiv. of this book.

I also return thanks to many Daffodil friends who have kindly refreshed my memory on various points, allowed me the use of photographs and rendered me other assistance.

The two pretty verses to "Mistress Daffodil" printed on page viii. are an extract from a charming little poem I heard some time ago. I am told by a good friend that the name of the talented authoress is Miss MARGARET JOHNSON, and that it appeared originally in the *Montreal Witness.*

It is hoped that no inconsistencies or inaccuracies in the use of botanical expressions will be found in this book, but the Reader is asked to remember that it is the work of one who is an enthusiastic *cultivator* of Daffodils, but not a professed botanist.

S. E. B.

CONTENTS

LIST OF ILLUSTRATIONS

xii

THE BOOK OF THE DAFFODIL.

CHAPTER I.

THE DAFFODIL, A MUCH VALUED FLOWER.

> . . . "The Narcissus wondrously glittering, a noble sight for all, whether immortal Gods, or mortal men; from whose root a hundred heads spring forth, and at the fragrant odour [thereof] all the broad heaven above, and all the earth laughed, and the salt-wave of the sea."
>
> "HYMN TO DEMETER."
>
> "Fed of heavenly dew the Narcissus blooms morn by morn with fair clusters, crown of the great goddesses from of yore."
>
> "ŒDIPUS AT COLONUS"—*Sophocles.*

IT is a flower we cannot do without, this Daffodil or Narcissus. Whether after the popular manner we adopt the prettier and more easily pronounced word and call it "Daffodil" (though "Daffodil" is really only a sectional name), or whether with more scientific people we keep to the well-established name of the genus and speak of it as the Narcissus, it is a plant which the ardent gardener feels he must grow as soon as he sees it in some of its finer forms.

It is a plant which has asserted itself much of late, and with good reason. Its numerous varieties supply a very real need in our gardens, and occupy a prominent position in the year's procession of beautiful flowers. Growing hardily in the open ground, they delight us at a time when cut flowers from the open border are very scarce; many of them rival in beauty the choicest treasures of the greenhouse and hot-house; with accom-

modating persistence they bloom in succession for nearly
a quarter of the year—*i.e.* (in ordinary seasons) from the
beginning of March to the middle of May—without
exacting from us any trouble and expense in supplying
them with artificial heat; when cut their flowers (most
of them) last in water for ten days, or even more; and
although there is a certain amount of truth in the objection that it is easy from a large collection to pick out a
number of sorts which are rather similar in character,
it is still easier to select a very large number which are
far more distinct from each other than rose from rose
and carnation from carnation. Their elegance, grace
and beauty are ravishing. The Narcissus may truly be
called the king of the spring garden, and all who have
a garden should do homage in his court, and at the same
time satisfy their own love of the beautiful by growing
a well-chosen collection.

In admiring the Narcissus we are in very good company, and in very ancient company too. Undoubtedly
known and prized from the earliest times all over the
south and east of Europe, and throughout North Africa,
and, as to the Tazetta section, to the farthest east, its
praises have been sung by the greatest poets of antiquity
from the time of Homer downwards.

In the "Hymn to Demeter" there is a fine description
of Narcissus Tazetta which is quoted at the head of this
chapter.

The same variety is described by Sophocles in his
"Œdipus at Colonus," as also quoted above.

Ovid recites the legendary story of the tragic death
of the beautiful youth Narcissus, how, as he lay on the
grass by the waterside, he had vainly fallen in love with
his own image reflected from the smooth surface of the
water; how he pined and died of his hopeless love, and
how the nymphs when they sought his body for burial
"only found a rising stalk with yellow blossoms

crowned." And Virgil in his fifth Eclogue alludes to Narcissus Poeticus as "purpureus Narcissus," "the brightly shining Narcissus," or (less probably) "the empurpled Narcissus."

But it was not only the theme of poets, it was in frequent use in old times as a decorative flower, and largely in connection with death and burial. That it was used before the Christian era in the making of funeral wreaths is known from the actual evidence of specimens of the Tazetta flower which, after long entombment, were unearthed in 1888, from an ancient cemetery at Hawara.

If we seek further proof of the way in which the Daffodil has entwined itself around the hearts of men and commended itself to them in their pleasures and sorrows, in their pensive and in their more joyous moods, we shall find such a proof in the long list of our English poets who have sung its praises—Green, Shakespeare, Spencer, Milton, Herrick, Keats, Shelley, Wordsworth and Tennyson, these are only a few of the great English singers with whom the Narcissus has been a household word.

As to the more practical side—viz., the history of its cultivation in gardens—the various kinds known to the older cultivators and the best methods of growing them are treated of by a very long series of writers both at home and abroad ever since the sixteenth century. We find these things mentioned or described in Turner's "Herbal" (1548); by Lobel (1570); by Clusius in his "Rariorum Stirpium Historiæ" (Antwerp, 1576), in which several species are described and figured; by Gerarde (1596) in his "Herbal," with descriptions of twenty-four different kinds all growing in his time in London gardens; by Parkinson (1629) in his "Paradisus Terrestris," in which descriptions and woodcuts are given of nearly a hundred varieties, and by many others.

4 THE BOOK OF THE DAFFODIL

In later times Dean Herbert in his "Amaryllidaceæ" (1837), and his contemporaries, Hawarth, Salisbury, Ellacombe and others, dealt with the characteristics and arrangement of the different forms and varieties of the plant.

But until quite recent times the love of the Daffodil and the knowledge of it as a *garden* flower was, with the large majority of people, confined to a few of the commoner sorts in cottage gardens or wild gardens and herbaceous borders. Then there arose a band of enthusiasts such as the Rev. C. Wolley Dod, Rev. W. Wilks, Messrs F. W. Burbidge, Peter Barr, Johnston, and Tait, Miss Ellen Willmott, the Rev. G. H. Engleheart, Messrs Bennett Pöe, Scrase-Dickins, J. C. Williams, James Walker, Dorrien-Smith, Hartland, De Graaff, the Rev. Arthur Boscawen, the Hon. J. Boscawen, Percy Williams, W. P. Milner, and many others who, as cultivators, students, collectors of wild forms and raisers of new seedlings, have rapidly enlarged and extended the knowledge and popularity of the plant. Fine varieties are now common enough. The Royal Horticultural Society has extended its fostering care to our flower, and other special Daffodil Societies have been formed. There are now choice Daffodil gardens in almost all parts of the country, and the time seems fast approaching when everyone who has any pretensions to be a gardener will grow some at least of the finer varieties.

The last work of importance dealing exclusively with the Daffodil is that by Mr F. W. Burbidge on "The Narcissus" (1875), which is full of interesting information and has been of the greatest value to Narcissus lovers, while Mr J. G. Baker's classification of the Narcissus in his "Amaryllideæ" (1888) evolved order where there was much confusion before, and is accepted as the standard authority at the present time.

NARCISSI IN ORCHARD

CHAPTER II.

THE different forms of the Narcissus are so numerous that it is impossible to grow even a small good collection intelligently and successfully unless we first get some clear ideas about the groups and divisions under which they are ranged. These depend chiefly upon the modifications in the structure of the flower bloom, although other characteristics such as the differences of colouring and of the habit and appearance of the foliage cannot be wholly ignored. Therefore before entering into the question of the best methods of cultivation, we must look at the structure of the Narcissus bloom and the bearing its variations have upon the classification of the genus.

If a flower of the common wild Daffodil, or of some other single trumpet Daffodil, say "Emperor," be bisected longitudinally by a clean cut beginning at the ovary and passing through its whole length, it will be seen to consist of two main parts—1st, a long tube; 2nd, a whorl of petal-like growths surrounding and enclosing a portion of this tube. The tube consists of two parts, viz., a short stumpy portion at the lower end extending from the ovary to the point where the whorl of petaloids bends away at an angle, this portion being called the perianth tube; and secondly, an outgrowth in prolongation of this perianth tube and about twice its length, which is called the corona or crown; this widens out as it goes until it ends in an open mouth, which is fringed

5

and slightly curved back at the edge.   If the mouth of
the crown be held downwards the whole tube is
somewhat of the shape and appearance of the skirt of a
lady's dress.

The second chiefly noticeable part of the flower is the
whorl of petal-like growths which surrounds the tube
on its outside, enclosing its coronal part.   This consists

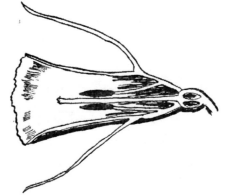

SECTION OF A TRUE DAFFODIL FLOWER.

of six divisions called perianth segments, as distinguished
from the perianth tube, though they are often more
loosely called the perianth.

These segments, in the flower we are examining, are
equal in length to the trumpet-like crown, and stand out
round it at an ascending angle a good deal less than
a right angle.   Within the tube will be seen the style
or thread-like prolongation of the ovary, and around it
six stamens ; these latter are all six of equal length, are

inserted in one set at the same point low down in the tube, stand away free from the side of the tube and reach halfway up the corona, the style being a little longer than the stamens.

If we now take a flower of the Pheasant's Eye Narcissus and bisect it as we did the other, we shall

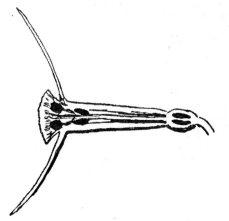

SECTION OF A TRUE NARCISSUS FLOWER.

find that though the two flowers are so different in appearance, the main features of their structure are generally the same, but that there is a considerable modification of the parts of this lastly bisected flower as compared with the flower of the Daffodil.

We still have a perianth tube, but now it is relatively very long instead of being short, it is slender and cylindrical instead of being stout and obconic. The

crown, inversely, is very short indeed, and is widely
expanded at about a right angle into a saucer-like shape.
The perianth segments, which enclose this small crown,
spread out widely and flatly at right angles to the tube
and are four or five times the length of the crown or
even more. The six stamens are divided into two sets
of three each, three being inserted near the mouth, the
other three at a point further down, below the crown,
but high up in the tube.

And now if flowers, say of the Incomparabilis or
Leedsii or Odorus groups be bisected, their structural
conformation will be found to be intermediate between
that of the two flowers already examined. The corona
will be neither of a trumpet nor saucer-like shape, but
in the form of a cup. The relative lengths of the
perianth tube, perianth segments, and crown, and the
width of angle which separates the segments from the
crown, will all be intermediate between those of the
Daffodil and the Pheasant's Eye flower. So too within
the tube, the position and other characteristics of the
stamens vary somewhat in different varieties, but will
be intermediate between those of the stamens of the
Daffodil and of the Poeticus flower.

It is upon such structural variations as these that
Mr Baker has based the classification of the Narcissus
which is now generally followed.

The whole genus is divided into three large groups,
according to the relative size of the corona. These are:—

I. The Magni-Coronati Group, made up, as the
name implies, of those smaller groups of Narcissi which
have *long crowns* or trumpets. These are the true
Daffodils.

II. The Medio-Coronati Group, made up of those
which have *crowns or cups of medium size.* These are
called Chalice-flowers or Star Narcissi.

III. The Parvi-Coronati Group, composed of those

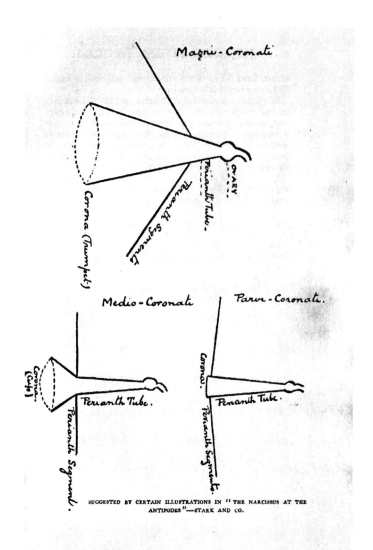

Magni - Coronati.

Ovary

Perianth Tube.

Perianth Segments

Corona (Trumpet)

Medio - Coronati

Corona (Cup)

Perianth Tube.

Perianth Segment.

Parvi - Coronati.

Corona.

Perianth Tube.

Perianth Segment.

SUGGESTED BY CERTAIN ILLUSTRATIONS IN " THE NARCISSUS AT THE
ANTIPODES "—STARK AND CO.

which have *short crowns* of a flat saucer-like shape. These are the true Narcissi.

In each of these groups a further natural division may be found between the species and varieties that have flat leaves, and those that have rush-like foliage. And in the first of these groups, and also in the Tazetta section of the third group, it is found convenient for practical purposes to make a rough and ready division, according to the differences of colouring.

For a fuller description and classification of the different forms belonging to each group, the reader is referred to the next chapter.

CHAPTER III.

THE divisions and sub-divisions of the Narcissus genus as given in this and the two following chapters follow generally Mr J. G. Baker's classification (" Amaryllideæ," 1888) but are not exactly the same in order of arrangement, or in every detail, and only those points are noted which seem especially useful to the cultivator, as distinct from the botanist. Other authorities have also been consulted, and some other matters introduced which are of interest to gardeners.

The whole genus Narcissus, as we have seen, falls into three large groups, according to the relative size of the crowns.[1]

The MAGNI-CORONATI (" Long-crowns"; also called Trumpet Narcissi, and True Daffodlls) have the crown cylindrical or funnel-shaped, and about as long, or even longer than the perianth segments, and the perianth tube correspondingly short.

The MEDIO-CORONATI (" Medium-crowns") are also called Star Narcissi and " Chalice-flowers"; and the divisional name, "Incomparable," is sometimes loosely applied to the whole group. They have the crown cup-shaped, about half as long as the perianth

---

[1] Those of the species and hybrids contained in the following lists which are best for garden cultivation, together with the best of the named garden hybrids, are particularised in chapter xii.

segments, though in some cases it is three-quarters as long, and in some (*e.g.* among the Barrii varieties) rather less than half as long.   They have the perianth tube relatively longer and narrower than the Magni-coronati.

The PARVI-CORONATI ("Short-crowns," or True Narcissi) have the crown obconic or saucer-shaped and less than half as long as the divisions of the perianth, and the perianth tube very slender, and very much longer than the crown.   Each of these larger groups has smaller groups under it.[1]

The MAGNI-CORONATI Group has two species—

(1) **Corbularia** (N. Bulbocodium) ("Hoop Petticoat" Daffodils).   From S. France, Spain, Portugal, Algeria and Morocco.   Chief distinguishing characteristics: the very insignificant spear-shaped perianth segments, the wide crinoline-shaped corona aad rounded rush-like leaves.   A small-growing species.   Best grown in cold frame or rock-work ; best varieties for cultivation, *conspicua* and *citrina*.   The Corbularias ripen seed abundantly and are more easily established from these than from bulbs.

Conspicua.   Spain.—Large yellow form ; height, six inches.

Præcox.   Spain.—Large early-flowering yellow ; height, six inches.

Tenuifolia.   Spain.—Small early-flowering golden ; height, three inches.

Var. GRAELSII.   Mountains of Castile.

---

[1] The descriptive lists in this and the two following chapters are arranged in three columns of different widths. In the widest column are placed the true species (printed in black-faced type) and the typical hybrids (in Italic capitals).   The sub-species and more important varieties (both in small capitals) are in a narrower inner column ; while in the right-hand and narrowest column of all are the less marked varieties (printed in *italics*) placed immediately after their types.

Pyrenean district. — Whitish, or primrose-yellow.

Var. MONOPHYLLA (or *Clusii*). Algiers.— White. Winter-flowering.

Var. CITRINA. S. France. — Sulphur-yellow. Rather larger than the type.

Var. NIVALIS. Mountains of Asturias and Central Spain, and in Portugal.—Deep yellow flowers.

(2) Ajax (**Pseudo-Narcissus**) (Trumpet Daffodils). A species having its home from Sweden and England to Portugal, Spain, Italy and Transylvania. Known by the long trumpet-like crown, oblong perianth segments, and flat bluish-green leaves. Cultivators, for convenience sake, generally divide this species with its six sub-species [see below] into three divisions, viz., *Self-yellow* Ajax, *Bicolor* Ajax, *White and Sulphur* Ajax. Under "*Self-yellow Ajax*" are ranged the various forms of the four sub-species, MAJOR, MINOR, MUTICUS, CYCLAMINEUS, and some of the connecting links *between Major and the type*. Under "*Bicolor Ajax*" come most of the forms of THE TYPE species, the sub-species BICOLOR, and connecting links *between the type and Moschatus*. Under "*White and Sulphur Ajax*" are placed the sub-species MOSCHATUS, and also the Pyrenean form of the type, *Pallidus Præcox*. In cultivation the *White Ajax* are delicate, the *Bicolors* easily grown. Of the *Self-yellow Ajax* some are uncertain, some very easily grown.

N.B.—The "long-crown" hybrids, resulting from various crosses between *N. Pseudo-Narcissus* and *N. Triandrus*, viz., the natural hybrid *N. Johnstoni*, and such garden hybrids as N. "Snowdrop," N. "Ada," etc., etc., seem to require more definite classification than they have yet received.

N. Johnstoni was originally described (AMARYLLIDEÆ, 1888) as a Portuguese form of *Pseudo-Narcissus*. But Mr Baker has now no doubt of its being from *Pseudo-Narcissus* × *Triandrus* [see MEDIOCORONATI, in chapter IV.]; and as it is of a very distinct and typical form, I venture to place it in a group to itself *as a typical hybrid*, and to range the various garden hybrids between *Pseudo-Narcissus* and *Triandrus* under this head as "JOHNSTONI."

Several of the varieties of *Pseudo-Narcissus* have double forms.

The recognised type flower of *Pseudo-Narcissus* is the wild Daffodil of England. Trumpet yellow; perianth segments pale sulphur. (White varieties of this are found here and there in Oxfordshire and Dorsetshire.)

There is a double form—

> *Gerard's Double Daffodil.*—(*N. Ps.-N. plenus.*)

Other forms are—

> *Scoticus* (the Scotch form), with a double form, *Scoticus plenus.*

> *Nobilis*, with both segments and mouth of trumpet more spreading.

> *Lobularis* (between the type and *Major*) with (*its supposed*) double forms, *Lobularis plenus* and *Grandiplenus.*

> *Cambricus.*— Sulphur - white perianth; yellow trumpet (between the type and *Major*).

> *Pallidus præcox.* — A pale sulphur-coloured, early-flowering form from S. France (Pyrenean district).

> *Rugilobus.*—Large primrose perianth; large yellow trumpet.

> *Variiformis.*—Pyrenean form between

MAGNI-CORONATI

(*A Pseudo-Narcissus form*)

SELF-YELLOW AJAX "EMPEROR"

Pseudo-Narcissus and *Moschatus* [Baker]. It has been ascribed to a cross between *Muticus* and some other form of *Pseudo-Narcissus*. Variable in size and shade of colour; white perianth; canary trumpet.

Princeps.—Probably of Italian origin.

Subsp. MAJOR.—Pyrenees and Spanish Peninsula. Self-yellow.—Larger in all its parts than the type.

Propinquus.—Larger form than *Major*. Bluer green in foliage.

Obvallaris (the Tenby Daffodil).—Very distinct form between *Major* and *Pseudo-Narcissus* type; medium size, wheel-like perianth; almost self-yellow.

Maximus. — Larger flower and more spreading rim to corona than in *Major*; the segments are twisted at ends; deep golden-yellow.

Spurius.—Hooded perianth, widely expanded trumpet-mouth.

Telamonius.—Form between *Major* and *Pseudo-Narcissus* type, having the large flower of the former and the sulphur-yellow perianth of the latter. The common double daffodil (*Telamonius plenus*) is its double form, which is quite distinct from another fine double Ajax with large rose-shaped flowers called *Plenissimus* (Parkinson's Rose-flowered Daffodil).

Lorifolius.—A form between *Major* and *Bicolor*. Perianth sulphur; trumpet yellow. To this type of flower belongs "*Emperor.*"

Subsp. MINOR. Pyrenees and Spanish Peninsula.—Self-yellow. Much smaller in all its parts than *Pseudo-Narcissus type*; about six inches high. Perianth segments gracefully twisted. It has a curious double form—" *Rip Van Winkle*."

Pumilus.—Somewhat more robust than *Minor*.

Minimus.—Very small in all its parts; otherwise generally resembling *Minor*. The smallest and earliest Trumpet Narcissus.

Nanus.—Flowers intermediate in size between those of *Minor* and *Minimus*, and having imbricated perianth segments.

Subsp. MUTICUS (Abscissus). Pyrenees.—Variable in form. Very thick, upright, dark-green leaves. Sulphury-yellow perianth; long narrow trumpet of full yellow, with clipt-off appearance at the mouth. The latest of all the wild trumpet forms.

Subsp. CYCLAMINEUS. Found near Oporto.—Very distinct, small drooping flower; perianth so much reflexed that the lemon-yellow segments are almost in a line with the long and deeper-yellow corona. Best grown in cold frames or rock-work, but likes moisture.

Subsp. BICOLOR. " Bicolor of Haworth," and of gardens, is not clearly known in a wild state and probably may have been a selection from either *Muticus* or *Variiformis*. Many fine garden varieties are traced to it. Sulphury-white perianth, spreading and imbricated, full yellow trumpet.

Subsp. MOSCHATUS. Pyrenees and Spanish Peninsula.—Flower variable in size; at first tinged with sulphur, but finally white. Segments as long as corona.

MAGNI-CORONATI

(*A. Johnstoni form*)

NATURAL HYBRID OF N. PSEUDO-NARCISSUS × N. TRIANDRUS

Albicans (called by the Dutch "*Mos-chatus*").— Larger flower, with more imbricated perianth segments.

Cernuus.—Perianth segments equal to and sometimes longer than trumpet. Medium size. More drooping and more squarely-built flower. It has two beautiful double forms — *Cernuus plenus* and *Cernuus plenus bicinctus.*

Tortuosus (" Leda," " Sarnian Belle ").— Perianth segments twisted, and shorter than trumpet.

(3) *N. JOHNSTONI.* A typical hybrid. Found wild in Portugal. (*Pseudo-Narcissus* × *Triandrus.*) Slightly variable in form. In colour from soft sulphur to pale lemon. Long, straight, funnel-shaped corona; perianth segments somewhat reflexed. Is best grown in grass or cold frames.

The best of the wild forms of this group are those which pass under the names—*Johnstoni type,* " Queen of Spain " and " Mrs George Cammell."

A number of beautiful garden hybrid *Johnstoni's* will be found among the CERTIFICATED VARIETIES enumerated in chap. xiii.

N. Triandrus [chap. iv.] also hybridises naturally with N. Bulbocodium (Corbularia).

NOTE.—A wild form between *N. Bulbocodium* and *Pseudo-Narcissus* was found by Messrs Tait and Barr in 1887, near Oporto.

CHAPTER IV.

THE second group — MEDIO-CORONATI—though made up chiefly of hybrids, contains two undoubted species and several wild hybrids until recently reckoned as species. In the following list the true species are put first, then the wild hybrids, then the ancient hybrids not now common in a wild state, and finally those typical garden hybrids of recent times to which so large a portion of our beautiful garden forms is to be referred.[1]

(1) **Triandrus.** Spain and Portugal.—Dwarf-growing, rush-leaved species. One to five flowered. Flowers variable in size. Cream-white perianth segments (equal in length to the tube), lance-shaped and sharply reflexed ; white chalice-shaped corona half as long as the segments.

Best grown in cold frame or rock-work ; requires well drained, gritty soil.

Concolor.—Pale self-yellow.

Pallidulus.—Primrose-yellow.

Pulchellus.—Segments yellow ; corona white.

Nutans.—Corona a deeper yellow than segments.

Subsp. CALATHINUS. From Isle of Glenans, Brittany. — Corona larger than in *Triandrus*, and about the same length as the reflexed

---

[1] See note chap. iii. p. 12.

perianth segments. Pale sulphur at first,
afterwards white. More beautiful even than
the type, and very rare.

> *Reflexus.*—Portuguese form connecting
> Calathinus with type.

(2) **Juncifolius.** Spain, Portugal and S. France.
—Very small species (the smallest Narcissus),
rush-leaved. One to four flowered (generally one
to three). Bright yellow flower; the spreading,
well-imbricated perianth segments about one-third
inch long, being about twice as long as the cup-
shaped corona which is often widely expanded. A
very variable plant. Best cultivated as recommended for *Triandrus.*

> Subsp. GADITANUS. — Flower smaller, the
> perianth segments being scarcely longer than
> the corona.
> Subsp. RUPICOLUS. — Very short pedicel;
> corona six-lobed and relatively small.
> Subsp. MINUTIFLORUS.—Very small; cut-
> short appearance in corona.
> Subsp. SCABERULUS.—Differs from the type
> chiefly in habit and leaf.

(3) *ODORUS* (Campernelle Jonquil). Portugal,
Spain, S. France and eastward to Italy and Dalmatia.
—Found wild but now reckoned as a hybrid, viz.,
Jonquilla × *Pseudo-Narcissus.* Bright green, rush-
like leaves; two to four (but generally two or
three) flowered. Flowers bright self-yellow;
perianth segments spreading, wedge-shaped, not
imbricated, about one inch long, being about twice
as long as the crown. There are two handsome
double forms ("*Queen Anne's Jonquils*"), which do
well in warm soils; one is rare.

> *Rugulosus,* with shorter and imbricated
> perianth segments; a more robust form.

Somewhat similar are Odorus *Calathinus* and *Interjectus*.

Var. MINOR.—Dwarf variety, with much smaller crown than any other form.

Var. LŒTUS (*Trilobus*). — Flowers smaller than *Campernelli*. Segments half as long again as the corona, which is much lobed.

Heminalis, a very distinct form, with long cup of darker yellow than the segments.

(4) *INCOMPARABILIS.* Wild over a considerable range from Spain and S.W. France to the Tyrol.—Very ancient hybrid (*Pseudo - Narcissus* × *Poeticus*) once reckoned as a species. But Dean Herbert raised a plant indistinguishable from it from the wild Yorkshire *Pseudo-Narcissus* × *Poeticus*, and many similar proofs have since been given. Leaves bluish - green; one flowered. Expanded flower, pale yellow in the type. Perianth segments spreading, slightly imbricated, about one and one-eighth inch long, being about twice as long as the crown.

The garden forms are very many and very various.

Concolor, segments and corona pale lemon - yellow. Of this class there are several fine garden varieties.

Semi-partitus differs from *Concolor* in the very deep lobing of its cup.

Albus plenus sulphureus ("Sulphur Phœnix," or "Codlins and Cream") is the supposed double form of *Semi-partitus*.

Var. AURANTIUS. — Perianth pale yellow; corona, yellow orange-stained.

Aurantius plenus ("Golden Phœnix,"

MEDIO-CORONATI
(*An Incomparabilis form*)
NARCISSUS "QUEEN ALEXANDRA"

"Butter and Eggs"), the well-known
double garden form.

Leedsii.—Corona rimmed with orange-
red. Many fine garden forms of this.

Var. ALBUS.—Perianth segments milk-white,
or very pale sulphur, corona lemon-yellow.
There are many fine garden forms after
this type.

Albus plenus aurantius ("Orange
Phœnix," "Eggs and Bacon"), well-
known double variety.

(5) *BERNARDI.*—Wild Pyrenean hybrid, varying much in form; said to grow wherever *Muticus*
(Abscissus) and *Poeticus* grow wild together, and
so found by Mr Peter Barr. Spreading white
perianth segments twice as long as the yellow cup,
which has something of the clipt appearance of *N.
Muticus.* In other respects the flower resembles
Incomparabilis. (Grenier, in "Flore de France,"
names and describes three forms of *Bernardi*,
two nearer *Pseudo-Narcissus* and one nearer to
Poeticus.)

Two specially fine collected forms,
"*Philip Hurt*" and "*H. E. Buxton*," have
very vivid red cups.

(6) *MONTANUS* (= *Poculiformis*). — Has been
known to cultivators for two centuries, and though
stated by Salisbury to be a native of damp Pyrenean
valleys, is thought by some to be an old garden
hybrid, as it cannot be matched by any wild form
now known. Dean Herbert suggested *Moschatus
× Dubius*, but it seems more probably from *White
Ajax × Poeticus*, and is really what in garden
hybrids we call a "*Leedsii.*" One to two flowered;
has pure white flowers, spreading perianth segments
about an inch long, rather imbricated, twice as long

as the white cup-shaped crown. Very beautiful when at its best, but seldom has perfect flowers.

(7) *MACLEAII.*—An old hybrid not found in a wild state. Origin unknown. Mr Baker considers it from *Pseudo-Narcissus Bicolor* × *Incomparabilis*. Mr Engleheart thinks it probably from some small, very stout form of *Bicolor* × *Poeticus*, but *possibly* from *Pseudo-Narcissus* × *Tazetta* (the bunch-flowered character having been lost). A small-growing Narcissus; one flowered; segments milk-white, much imbricated, about three-quarter inch long; corona bright yellow, about half inch long. Received from France (1819) by Mr Alex. Macleay and named after him.

> *Sabini*, of similar parentage but more robust, with larger flowers and corona longer in proportion to the segments.

(8) *NELSONI.*—A garden type, having considerable resemblance to *Macleaii*, but much more robust. White segments, one to one and a half inches long, much imbricated, lemon-yellow crown more than half as long as the segments. Its parentage seems probably to be *Bicolor* × *Poeticus*, from which cross Mr Engleheart has raised numerous hybrids closely similar to it as well as flowers of *Incomparabilis* and *Backhousei* character.

> There are many garden forms of this, one of which, *Nelsoni Aurantius*, is very conspicuous for the remarkably vivid orange-red colour of the cup.

(9) *BACKHOUSEI.*—Garden hybrid raised by Mr W. Backhouse of St John's, Weardale. Mr Baker thinks this *Pseudo-Narcissus* × *Incomparabilis*. It has also been ascribed to *Pseudo-Narcissus* × *Tazetta*. But Mr Engleheart has raised *Backhousei* forms as well as *Nelsoni* from *Bicolor* × *Poeticus*. Peri-

MEDIO-CORONATI
(*A Leedsii form*)
NARCISSUS "LILIAN"

anth segments sulphur-yellow, imbricated, spreading horizontally, and about one to one and a quarter inches long; corona, lemon-yellow, nearly equals the segments in length.

Several named forms are in cultivation.

(10) *TRIDYMUS*. (*Pseudo-Narcissus × Tazetta*). —Two to three flowered, the flowers being in shape somewhat like those of *Nelsoni*, but smaller.

There are several named forms (most of them yellow) in cultivation.

(11) *HUMEI*.—Garden hybrid raised by Dr Leeds of Manchester, said to be between *Pseudo-Narcissus* and *Montanus*. One flowered. Sulphur-yellow segments about one and a half inches long, loosely ascending; corona, lemon-yellow, about an inch long. The flower has a deformed, clipt-off appearance.

> *Concolor*, with umbrella-like lemon perianth segments, and straight well-formed cup of rather darker shade. The only form worth growing.
>
> Var. *Albidus*.—Small form with milk-white segments and lemon-yellow crown. A deformed flower.

(12) *LEEDSII*.—Garden hybrid raised by Dr Leeds. One flowered. Flowers slightly drooping. Spreading perianth segments, milk-white, about one to one and a quarter inches long; cup-shaped corona of very pale yellow, about half an inch long. In most of the forms of the Leedsii group the cup passes off white. The leaves of many of the forms are twisted.

The *Leedsii* varieties are the result of crossing the delicate *White Ajax* varieties with *Poeticus*, and to many of them the *Poeticus* blood gives considerable robustness of constitution.

There are many fine named forms, ranking among the most beautiful of the Star Narcissi.

(13) *BARRII.*—Garden hybrid raised by Mr W. Backhouse. "Covers a series of forms intermediate between *Incomparabilis* and *Poeticus*, but nearer the former than the latter." *Poeticus* × *Pseudo - Narcissus.* One flowered. Spreading perianth segments of sulphur-yellow, slightly imbricated, about one to one and a quarter inches long, being twice or more than twice the length of the short and rather expanded crown, which is yellow throughout in the type, but in most of the forms now cultivated is margined with red or orange.

N.B.—*N. Incomparabilis* × *N. Poeticus* will yield forms of the *Barrii* group as well as of *Burbidgei.* Many named forms of great beauty.

NOTE.—Other hybrids less interesting to the gardener are omitted.

CHAPTER V.

THE Parvi-coronati group contains seven species which are placed first in the following arrangement, the wild hybrids come next, and last the garden hybrids.

(1) **N. Poeticus** (Pheasant's Eye Narcissus). Species widely distributed in Europe, all through the Mediterranean region from France to Greece. Flat glaucous leaves; flower solitary; perianth segments pure white, spreading and imbricated; the yellow crown saucer-shaped, with deep-red, much crisped edge. The type, a tall and very shapely flower of middle size, blooms in May.

Narcissus Poeticus naturally falls into two sections—the early flowering (March and April), and late flowering (May). A new section of large and fine-flowered garden forms has arisen of late years by cross-fertilisation between various individuals of the species.

Early flowerers.

ANGUSTIFOLIUS (*radiiflorus*); a sub-species; the earliest in flower; of fragile habit; has very narrow perianth segments.

Grandiflorus præcox, finely formed; after style of the later "*Recurvus*," but much less recurved in the segments.

Ornatus, which flowers a few days after

25

"*Grandiflorus præcox*"; distinct and of perfect shape, having broad, rounded, imbricated perianth segments of excellent substance.   Probably of Italian origin.

Poetarum; flowers very shortly after *Ornatus*.   Has perianth segments slightly recurved and the crown not merely edged but suffused throughout with bright red.

Grandiflorus, very large flowered variety with floppy perianth segments.

Tripodalis, with rather narrow and reflexing segments.

Late flowerers.

THE TYPE (*Poeticus of Linnæus*).

Recurvus, with slightly imbricated and recurving perianth segments, and much recurving leaves.

Stellaris, distinguished by its inch-long bladder-like distended spathe.

Patellaris has a flat, finely-formed, much imbricated perianth and large crown.

Verbanensis, a small, graceful, dwarf-growing variety with rather narrow and reflexing segments; connected with sub-species *Angustifolius*.

Poeticus plenus, the common double ("Gardenia flowered") Narcissus, flowering as late as June.   Supposed to be the double form of "*Patellaris*." There is a smaller form which is probably the double of *Poeticus* of Linnæus (the type).

(2) **N. Jonquilla.**[1]   A species found in Spain,

[1] See footnote, chap. iii. p. 12.

PARVI-CORONATI
(*A Poeticus form*)

France, through Italy to Dalmatia, and in Algeria.
Long, bright-green, rush-like leaves, deeply chan-
nelled down the middle; two to six flowered;
bright self-yellow flowers; perianth segments
spreading and scarcely imbricated, three or four
times as long as the saucer-shaped crown. Varies
in habit, but is readily distinguished from *Odorus*
by its narrower segments and flatter crown, and
from *Juncifolius* by its much larger size and relatively small crown. Does well in a warm, open
border in rich soil.

The double form, *Jonquilla flore pleno*,
rarely does well in the open border, but
is very fine under glass.

VAR. MINOR, dwarf form from south of Spain
and Algeria.

VAR. STELLARIS with perianth segments
lance-shaped and reflexing.

Sub-species—JONQUILLOIDES. Crown more
than half as long as the segments, which are
imbricated.

(3) **N. Tazetta** (*Polyanthus Narcissus*). A
species remarkable for its great variability, and
also for its very widely extended geographical
distribution—viz., from the Canary Isles and Portugal through S. Europe and N. Africa to Syria,
Persia, Cashmere, India, as far as China and Japan.
Has long been naturalised in the mild climate of
the Scilly Isles and Cornwall. Flat glaucous
leaves. Usually four to eight flowered in the
type. Perianth segments white, imbricated and
spreading horizontally; the shallow cup-shaped
crown yellow and small relatively to the segments.
This species is probably the Narcissus of the
Greek classical writers.

Its sub-species (which cannot be particularly described here) are very numerous, the chief of them (as arranged by Mr Baker) being :—

(1) *Bicolors* (perianth segments white, corona yellow).

LACTICOLOR, CORCYRENSIS, PATULUS, OCHROLEUCUS.

(2) *White Tazettas* (segments and crown both white).

PAPYRACEUS, PANIZZIANUS, DUBIUS, CANARIENSIS, PACHYBOLBOS, POLYANTHOS.

(3) *Yellow Tazettas* (segments and crown both yellow).

ITALICUS, BERTOLONII, AUREUS, CUPULARIS.

A list of forms specially suitable for cultivation will be found in chapter ix.

(4) **N. Viridiflorus.**—A singular autumn-flowering species. Found in Morocco and Gibraltar, where it flowers in November. Rush-like foliage, one to four flowered. Both perianth and crown green, the crown being very small. Practically impossible of cultivation in English gardens.

(5) **N. Serotinus.**—Autumn-flowering species. Spain, through coasts of the Mediterranean to the Holy Land. Very slender rush-like foliage, which is not produced until the flowers are over. Flower generally solitary, rarely two flowered. Perianth segments spreading, pure white, with tendency to become reflexed; small lemon-yellow crown. Very difficult of cultivation in this country; impossible unless the leaves, which are produced very late, are sheltered from early frosts.

Var. DEFICIENS has scarcely any corona.

(6) **N. Elegans.**—Autumn-flowering species. Sicily, Italy and Algiers. Slender rush-like foliage, two to six flowered (usually two to four). Perianth

segments pure white, spreading and very acute;
saucer-shaped yellow crown. Much resembles
"*Serotinus*" in general habit, although it differs in
bearing more flowers, in the greater slenderness of
its segments, and in producing its leaves at the
same time as its flowers. Not at all suited for
cultivation here.

Var.: OBSOLETUS has rather broader segments, and crown nearly obsolete.

(7) N. Broussonetii. A unique species which,
after being long lost, was some few years ago dis-
covered by Dr Leared and others in Morocco. Flat-
leaved; many-flowered. The pure white flower is
somewhat bell-shaped, and the crown is reduced to
a mere rim. This remarkable plant may possibly
have had its origin in a cross between Narcissus
and some other Amaryllidaceous plant belonging to
a different genus.

(8) *N. BIFLORUS.* Probably a natural hybrid
between *Tazetta* and *Poeticus,* its home being France,
Switzerland, Italy and the Tyrol; it is semi-wild in
England (being found in Devonshire) and Ireland.
Some view it as a species. It has been called the
"Northern and extreme form of *Tazetta* as it approaches *Poeticus.*" Flat-leaved, flowers usually
two, sometimes one, seldom three. " May be described as *N. Poeticus* with two flowers on a scape,
and a yellow cup minus the purple rim." It flowers
in England in May. The perianth segments are
milky-white, or very pale primrose (hence its old
name " Primrose Peerless Daffodil "), with a small
crown, yellow, and less-spreading than in *Poeticus.*
The scent, according to Parkinson, is " sweet, but
stuffing."

There are several varieties intermediate between the type and *N. Poeticus,* of which *N.*

Biflorus Albus has segments of snowy-white and the corona tinged with red.

(9) *N. ORIENTALIS.* Probably a hybrid between *Incomparabilis* and *Tazetta.* Flat-leaved; three to four flowered; the spreading segments of sulphur-yellow three times as long as the orange-yellow cup-shaped corona.

(10) *N. INTERMEDIUS.* A hybrid supposed to be between some form of *Tazetta* and *Jonquilla.* Found in Spain, Balearic Isles and S. of France; abundant on the hills near Bayonne and the Landes of Dax. Differs from the yellow-flowered Tazettas by its sub-cylindrical deep-green leaves; is many-flowered; cup about one-fourth or fifth the length of the perianth segments; the whole flower being of a soft yellow colour.

> Intermedius *Bifrons* has narrower perianth segments and a deeper corona. A very beautiful garden form of this with orange-scarlet cup is *Bifrons* "Sunset." Other forms are *Bicrenatus* and *Primulinus* and *Radiatus.*

(11) *N. GRACILIS.* An old garden plant, said to have been found wild near Bordeaux, but not generally met with in a wild state. Supposed to be *Jonquilla* × *Tazetta*, or (by some) *Juncifolius* × *Tazetta.* Rush-leaved; one to three flowered. Full yellow flower, changing to pale sulphur; perianth segments spreading and imbricated; very late in flower.

> *Tenuior* (the "Silver Jonquil"), a much paler form, and more slender in all its parts.

(12) *N. BURBIDGEI.* This group name "covers a series of forms between *Incomparabilis* and *Poeticus* in which the characters of the latter predominate"

PARVI-CORONATI
(*A Burbidgei form*)
NARCISSUS "INCOGNITA"

(J. G. Baker). "Most of the true Burbidgei's are merely seminal phases of N. Poeticus, the Daffodil parentage being almost if not quite obliterated" (F. W. Burbidge). *Burbidgei* (type) has pure white segments spreading horizontally and inclined to reflex, and a small yellow crown suffused and edged very bright red.

There is a considerable variety, both in colour and outline, among the forms usually classed as Burbidgei; and some more accurate rule than at present obtains is needed for distinguishing between these and flowers of the Barrii group.

CHAPTER VI.

The cultivation of the Narcissus or Daffodil is not difficult, but in this, as in most things, there are differences of opinion; so, for the assistance of those who at present know little or nothing about the matter, I shall lay down a few easy rules which, in my own experience, I have found sufficient to secure a very satisfactory measure of success.

But before coming to these special rules, let me insist very strongly upon some general principles of good gardening, which are of marked importance in Narcissus cultivation.

(1) Everything should be done *thoroughly*; let there be no shirking of labour, let there be no hurried and superficial work. (2) Everything should be done *at the right time*. With our English climate we can hardly ever make quite sure of being able to do to-morrow any item of garden work which ought to have been done to-day. (3) Every plant grown should be put as far as is possible into *suitable surroundings*. You cannot expect good results if you try to grow things under conditions which are not congenial to their nature. (4) Garden work should be *in the future* as well as in the present, *i.e.* there should be definite and well thought out plans of work to be done later on, such as planting, lifting, rearranging beds, exhibiting, etc., and careful preparation should be made beforehand, so as to be ready to do each kind of work promptly, when the

32

proper time comes. (5) There should be a sensible
system of labelling which should be carried out carefully,
so that the names of the plants you value may not be
lost by the perishing of the labels themselves, or the
obliteration of the writing upon them.

Now for the special rules, and

(1) As to Soil.—The greater number of varieties
will do very fairly well in almost any kind of garden
soil, but even the most accommodating kinds will of course
produce their best results when grown in the most
suitable surroundings.   It is often stated that the
Narcissus does best in strong soil.   But such a state-
ment is misleading when made without modification.
Let me tell my own experience, reaching over a good
many years, with a large and representative collection.
I began growing Narcissi in a garden of very good but
decidedly strong loam, and inclined to be wet in winter.
The soil was rather shallow, varying from eleven to
fourteen inches in depth, and resting on a sub-soil of
strong clay.   I got exceptionally fine flowers, but many of
the plants "went off," and I found at lifting time a large
number of bulbs affected with "basal rot" [see chap. x.].
I was told I must expect heavy losses of this kind in
Narcissus growing, but the percentage seemed too high.
Accordingly, I made a number of deep, well-drained
beds, and mixed a lot of lighter soil with the
natural soil of the garden, and worked in a plentiful
supply of "wood-ashes" before planting.   In these
beds I planted delicate and doubtful kinds, and the
more expensive bulbs of vigorous kinds, and put the
white Daffodils and some other very delicate kinds in
maiden loam of a rather light and gritty character.   The
result has been delightful, and for years past my
Narcissi have not only given me excellent flowers (not
quite so large perhaps in some cases as in the heavy
soil, but still very excellent, and year by year maintain-

ing their excellence), but also an unusually small proportion of unhealthy bulbs. So I recommend a not too heavy loam—a well-drained soil of medium consistency, with a certain character of grittiness—as the best all round soil for Narcissi. The particular constitutions, however, of the different groups should be considered as much as possible. The Poeticus and Burbidgei varieties, with almost all the Star Narcissi and a few of the stronger Daffodils (such as " Emperor," and the stronger kinds of Bicolors) produce their best results in good, fairly strong, moist loam; the more delicate varieties in a medium soil, inclining to light (sandy, gravelly, or stony). The White Trumpet Daffodils, most beautiful of all the Narcissi, and among the most uncertain, with some of the more uncertain kinds of self-yellow Daffodils (especially those of *Spurius* blood, also *Maximus* and *Minor*), do best in maiden turfy loam, and soon become diseased in soil that has much humus in it. Heavy beds should be mixed with rock gravel or some other gritty material. The White Daffodils also do well in soil that has some peat.

(2) AS TO SITUATION AND POSITION.—Of course it is delightful in spring to see the bright cheery flowers of the Narcissus in large irregularly shaped masses in the hardy flower borders, and cheap bulbs of strong, good kinds may well be planted in such a position. Such strong and inexpensive kinds may also be grown in beds in the front garden, arranged in clumps at such a distance every way as shall leave room for planting half hardy annuals between them. This will make the beds gay with flowers later on during the summer months. It will not be advisable of course to use choice kinds for such a purpose, and when any such plan is adopted, it will be necessary to keep the bed in good heart by giving a surface mulching of well decomposed stable manure every year. The better kinds, however,

deserve to be grown in a place to themselves, where
they can be properly studied and attended to. But beds
given up to them entirely in the front garden will be
untidy while the leaves are dying off, and empty during
the summer and autumn.   It is a good plan, therefore,
to assign to the Narcissi some portions of ground in
suitable parts of the kitchen garden. Long rectangular
beds are the most convenient, made four feet wide, so that
it is easy to reach to the middle from either side,
without setting foot upon them.   I enclose mine with
wood edging boards which have been well tarred.
This not only prevents the edges of the bed getting
trampled upon, but makes it easy to raise the level a
few inches above the surrounding surface, which is *a
very beneficial arrangement* in gardens inclined to be wet.
The more vigorous varieties will do well with almost
any aspect which is not absolutely sunless ; but sunshine
is necessary to properly ripen the leaves while the next
year's flowers are forming, and so any bulbs that are
planted in a very shady place should not be allowed
to remain unmoved more than one or at the most two
seasons.   Undoubtedly Narcissi prefer to have a fair
amount of sunshine, but to be partially shaded from the
midday sun.   The White Daffodils are particularly
grateful for the shade of trees, as long as the sun is
not wholly kept from them, and these varieties do
much better when planted near to (but not immediately
under) a hedge or shrubs.   They then have to maintain
a contest with the fibrous roots of their encroaching
neighbour, and their health is best when they have to
fight for their living.   Wherever your beds may be
placed, let the ground be deeply dug (I prefer it double
trenched), and well drained, if there is not good natural
drainage.   But the digging should be done long enough
before planting time (say two or three weeks) to let the
soil settle, for the Narcissus does not like to be planted

in loose soil. If for any reason you are obliged to pre-
pare your beds in summer *shortly* before planting time,
it is a good and simple plan to take some opportunity
when the soil is not wet and press them down firmly
by placing a fairly wide board on the surface and
standing upon it. This very primitive method gives an
even and not too great pressure, and will relieve you
from the necessity of planting in too loose soil.

Though the Narcissus likes plenty of moisture when
it is in vigorous growth, it likes that moisture to pass
through, and not remain stagnant in the soil ; and the
bulbs of most of the varieties strongly resent being
water-logged, in fact they soon get diseased under such
a condition. Those bulbs which are in deeply dug beds
do better both in dry and in wet seasons than those
planted in shallow soil. A good deal must, of course,
depend on the nature of the subsoil, but as a general
rule deep digging and good drainage are necessary to
permanent success.

In the case of *very dry and sandy soils, when the natural
drainage is free*, it may be found advantageous to place a
layer of stable manure at a depth of at least 12 inches,
so as to be quite out of reach of the bulbs ; it should
not be mixed with the soil but be merely a *layer*, as it is not
intended for a stimulant (which would be injurious to
many of the varieties) but only as a sponge to retain
moisture in the soil.

GROWING IN GRASS.—Almost all Narcissi look well
and do well planted in grass, if you can spare them a
corner of a lawn or meadow which can be left without
mowing until the end of June. For the Narcissus leaves
must not be cut, but left to die naturally. Any of the
delicate sorts, which you cannot induce to grow happily
in cultivated beds, may be dibbled into the grass in
holes, filled up with maiden loam, and left to themselves. They should not be planted stiffly, but in

NARCISSUS POETICUS RECURVUS IN GRASS

irregularly shaped patches—each sort in a clump to itself—and with sufficient room left between the bulbs for their gradual increase. The flowers will not be so large as in the border, and the bulbs will make very slow increase, but they will be more healthy and happy. They do well on turfy bosses at the roots of trees. Another excellent situation for planting is by the water-side, on the margins of lakes or streams. This position is a very natural one for the Narcissus and has often been noted by the poets when describing our flower. So Shelley—" And Narcissi, the fairest among them all, who gaze on their eyes in the stream's recess, till they die of their own dear loveliness."

But what position is there in which—given only the right soil and other conditions suitable for them—these beautiful flowers do not show themselves to advantage ?

> " On meadow green, by leafy hedge,
> In woodland shade, and rushy sedge,
> By little lowly rills ;
> While yet the North wind blows his blast,
> Before the storm and sleet are past,
> Laugh out the Daffodils."

Exeter Flying Post.

CHAPTER VII.

As to Planting.—There is a rooted conviction in the minds of some old-fashioned gardeners that Guy Fawkes' Day is about the proper time for planting Narcissus bulbs. But this is two or three months too late *if you wish to secure the best results.* Of course November-planted bulbs will produce flowers; you may get flowers —of a kind—even from bulbs planted in January. But to get the most vigorous plants, the most perfect flowers, the greatest possible increase of bulbs, you *must plant early.* In August (and often quite early in August) a ring-like swelling may be seen all round the base of the bulb. This is caused by the effort of the young roots to start into growth, and it is Nature's warning to plant the bulbs as soon as you can if you do not wish them to lose in vigour. The amateur should therefore order his bulbs early, and make a point of getting them early; and should plant them as soon as he receives them. The Poeticus varieties need planting first, for they have no period of rest; then the Burbidgei; then, as a rule, the Star Narcissi; then, with some exceptions, the Daffodils; in fact a good general rule is that the more Poeticus blood there is in the bulbs the sooner they need planting. Exceptions to the rule are—the *Tenby* Daffodil, and *Maximus*, and the *Spurius* varieties (including the popular "Henry Irving" and "Golden Spur"), which are all much better for being planted among the earliest; and some kinds, like Bicolor "Horsfield," show, by the

38

tendency of their bulbs to shrink and get very dry soon when kept out of the ground, that they should be early replanted. It is most desirable to get Poeticus varieties in the ground by the end of July, and the whole stock by the end of August. Early planting is, there can hardly be a doubt, essential *if the best results are to be secured.*

A change of soil and locality is highly beneficial to the Narcissus; and though few people are fortunate enough to have two gardens in different localities, much can be done in the way of changing the soil of Narcissus beds by digging in from time to time soil of a different character. The beds should also be fallowed from time to time, and different kinds of crops taken from them; and when old beds have to be replanted at once without rest or change, there is some advantage to be gained by growing Daffodils where the other sorts of Narcissi have previously stood, and *vice versa.*

When fine flowers and fine bulbs are wanted, rather than general decorative effect, the bulbs should, where possible, be planted in rows north and south, the rows being a foot apart, and the bulbs planted from three to six inches from each other in the rows, according to size (and even a little further apart in the case of exceptionally large bulbs, such as "Emperor" and "Sir Watkin"). This gives them ample room to stand for two or three years before lifting again. When there is shortness of room the planting may be closer than is recommended; but it is better for securing both good flowers and fine bulbs to give the extra space, for the plants are much benefited by having plenty of air and light, and the foot space between the rows makes it easy to keep the ground open with a small hoe, a very beneficial operation, both in autumn and again when the plants are coming through the ground in spring. Here, again, as in the matter of soil and position, the White

Trumpet Daffodils require rather exceptional treatment; they do best planted very closely in their rows, in fact, almost touching one another.

The depth at which a Narcissus bulb should be planted varies according to its size and according to the nature of the soil. The depth of soil above the neck of the bulb—the neck is that part near the top where the bulb begins to swell out into its ovoid form—should be one and a half times the depth of the bulb itself. This gives an average covering of from two to three inches of soil; but in very heavy soils the depth of planting should be a little less, in very light soils the bulbs may be planted a little deeper. In the case of the glorious but somewhat uncertain Daffodil "Maximus" deep planting answers best. More and finer flowers are thus obtained than by planting it at the usual depth.

Planting should be done, if possible, when the soil is nicely damp (not wet), and in planting great care should be taken to settle the base of the bulb firmly in the soil, so that no air space is left under it. In my own practice in a garden inclined to be wet I generally, when bulbs are planted in fairly strong soil, put a little coarse silver sand both under and over the choicer kinds, and I do so with delicate kinds even in the lighter soil. This proves very beneficial in wet seasons, and there has been no disadvantage from it even in the driest. There are some authorities who discourage this practice; but circumstances of soil alter cases, and experience only can teach what is most suitable in each case.

After planting, the surface of the beds should be kept open by "lightening up" with a hand fork about every ten days or fortnight throughout the autumn; otherwise it will become too hard set by the autumn rains.

When planted the bulbs should in general be left undisturbed for two seasons. Varieties which increase slowly may, if they seem quite happy, be left for three

MAGNI-CORONATI
(*A Pseudo-Narcissus form*)
SELF-YELLOW AJAX MAXIMUS

years; and on the other hand, delicate sorts which look as if they were not doing well, may, with advantage, be lifted year by year.   But too frequent lifting and too greedy subdivision of the bulbs is not desirable as a rule, and indeed, may be the cause of injury in some cases one hears of, in which varieties of strong constitution like "Horsfield" have begun to develop weakness.

As to Nourishment.—Narcissus growers have had some trouble and differences of opinion in deciding how they may best supply their bulbs with the necessary nourishment.   One rule now seems to be pretty generally admitted.   No stable manure should be dug into the ground for some time before planting; even the most vigorous varieties do not like such manure to be in contact with their bulbs and roots.   But most varieties may be planted with advantage in ground from which early potatoes (or such like crops) have been taken, for in this case the rawness and much of the strength of the manure have departed before the bulbs have anything to do with it.   And the ground will be in still more favourable condition if the year before the potato crop it has been well prepared and used for celery or peas, and then thrown up roughly to the action of the frost during the winter.   Thoroughly prepared in this way and then cropped with potatoes, it will be in admirable order for Narcissi.

No better plan can be suggested for the renovation of Narcissus beds than to dig in a plentiful supply of well-rotted turfy soil (when such is obtainable), particularly that of a dark-yellow or red-brown colour, with iron in it, and "wood-ashes" are very valuable thoroughly mixed with the soil before planting.   When it is necessary to apply manure our guiding rule must be that the Daffodil likes phosphates, but strongly objects to ammonia.   Basic slag and crushed bones and dissolved bones seem to be the most reliable manures.   These in the opinion of some experts may be mixed with the soil and placed next the bulbs at planting time, but a better plan seems to be to apply them as a top dressing soon after planting, mixing them in with a hand fork in the covering of soil above the bulbs but not in immediate contact with them.   Half a pound of basic slag, or one and a half to two ounces of dissolved bones to each square yard, or an equivalent in bone meal, is probably the best prescription.   When beds of *strong growing* varieties and clumps of them in borders need fresh nourishment, they may with advantage be mulched early in the autumn with a dressing of thoroughly decayed manure through which the leaves will find their way in due course.   It will be useful to remember with regard both to manure and strong loam that the more Poeticus blood there is in any variety the better will it enjoy strength of food and soil.

MAGNI-CORONATI

(*A Pseudo-Narcissus form*)

SELF-YELLOW AJAX "KING ALFRED"

CHAPTER VIII.

GATHERING THE FLOWERS—LIFTING THE BULBS.

As to Gathering the Flowers.—If the greatest possible enjoyment is to be obtained from the cut flowers of the Narcissus they should not be left on the plant until fully opened, at the mercy of wind, rain, sun and dust, but cut as soon as the perianth begins to unwrap itself from the crown, and then allowed to open out in water in a fairly warm room, or other sheltered place, such as a greenhouse. All the beauty and freshness of colour which are so charming in the Narcissus will thus be preserved; and although flowers which have been open on the plant for a considerable time may attain to a rather larger size, the slight gain in this respect does not counterbalance the loss in purity and freshness. A further advantage gained is that flowers cut in the bud may be packed for travelling in a much smaller space, and yet will open out in water better and even larger than flowers cut as soon as they have quite opened out on the plant. *Pœticus recurvus,* the late Pheasant's Eye flower, may be gathered even before the spathe has burst, but *Pœticus ornatus* and the *Burbidge's* should not be cut until the spathe has burst and the bud turned; while the Trumpet varieties should wait until the perianth has partly separated itself from the crown.

The cut flowers never look so graceful as when arranged with their own foliage; but as cutting the leaves injures or destroys the bulbs, patches of the common sorts should be grown in quantity, ensuring a supply of leaves to set off the flowers of the choicer kinds.

43

Narcissus flowers look much better when the contents of each vase or glass are of one variety only, and the best kind of glasses for drawing-room and table decoration are cylindrical, as much as possible like a rose specimen tube in shape, but in various sizes to suit the different lengths of the flower stalks.

As to Lifting the Bulbs.—After one, two, or three years, as the case may be, the bulbs must be taken up and the off-sets they have produced separated from them, and it is even more important to be right in the time of lifting than in the time of planting. It is, I believe, to errors in lifting that we may trace many of the failures, or half-successes, which are sometimes complained of in the cultivation of Narcissi. The rule laid down for me years ago by an expert grower was this—in the matter of lifting *better be too early than too late*. My own experience has amply borne out this rule. Some of the varieties have no period of bulb rest, *i.e.* they begin to put out the roots for their new season's growth before the old season's foliage has begun to die away. This is especially the case with the Poeticus varieties—but it is not confined to them—and those varieties which do rest, rest only for a short time. Now, if the bulbs be lifted after new rootlets have been put forth these new roots, unless the bulbs be immediately replanted, must die off, and the vigour of the bulb will be diminished. In the case of delicate sorts, or where much new growth has taken place, the consequences may be most serious, the constitution of the bulb permanently injured. There is a great temptation to leave the bulbs in the ground until the foliage has quite died down, for they are much more easy to handle when taken up late in this way; and, besides, it is not always convenient to attend to them at the right time. But it is really of very great importance to stick to the rule, " better too early than too late." If you should take up the bulb a little too early no real harm is done; the flower may be a little smaller the following year, but the bulb will be healthy; but if you are too late the consequences may be disastrous.

Only experience and experiment can teach how soon fresh root growth is to be expected in any particular variety. But the *Poeticus* varieties, *Maximus* and *Odorus* require to be lifted before they show any sign of fading foliage. For most of the other sorts the safe rule is "*as soon as possible after the fading of the leaves has decidedly set in*"—to be still more definite—as soon as the upper third part of the leaves has turned yellow.

When the bulbs are lifted the offsets of the commoner sorts may generally be separated by carefully pulling apart; but this is too rough-and-ready a plan for dividing the less forward offsets of the more valuable kinds. In the case of these, any small portion of the base which still connects the offsets with the mother bulb should be cut through with a sharp knife, and it is better not to separate any bulbs where there is danger of cutting any part of the bulb except the base.

If the sun is shining when the bulbs are being lifted they should be placed at once in shade, as the sudden change from the cooler soil into hot sunshine is calculated to act injuriously upon them. There are differences of practice here, but I find the opinion of several experienced growers to coincide with my own. The objection of increased trouble does not justify carelessness in this matter if, as I believe, ultimate injury may result from it.

The bulbs, after being lifted, should be spread out to dry in some cool airy place; and in storing them away after drying until replanting begins, it is better to keep them spread out in shallow trays, not heaped up one upon another. Trouble and labour expended on such details will bring their own reward in securing the general excellence of the stock.

CHAPTER IX.

CULTIVATION IN COLD FRAMES.—With careful cultivation even finer flowers of some of the varieties may be obtained from bulbs grown in boxes and pots in well protected cold frames than will be generally produced by the same varieties outside, and there will be a little gain also in severe seasons in the earliness of flowering. Most kinds lend themselves to such treatment, but the following may be mentioned as being particularly useful for the purpose :—*Tenby* (obvallaris), *Henry Irving, Pallidus præcox, Albicans, Cernuus, Telamonius plenus, Princeps,* Johnstoni *Queen of Spain, Victoria, Emperor, Queen Bess, Sir Watkin, Minnie Hume, Barrii conspicuus, Macleaii, Ornatus, Tenuior,* Intermedius *Sunset* (all these in boxes). Also the small growing kinds :—*Minimus, Corbularia conspicua* and *citrina, Cyclamineus, Triandrus albus, Juncifolius* and *Minor* (in pots and pans). Others, of course, may be added.

The results will depend on the attention given to details, and some advice is now given for those who have not as yet had experience in this kind of plant growing. For the deeper rooting kinds strong wooden boxes can be obtained from any grocer, about seven inches deep by eight inches wide and twenty inches long. Make holes for drainage. Put some lumps of charcoal at the bottom, cover them with a layer of half-rotten turf and fill with a mixture of good fibrous loam

MEDIO CORONATI
(*A Leedsii form*)
NARCISSUS "MINNIE HUME"

and good sandy and gritty soil and a little wood ashes ;
and in the boxes for strong-growing sorts (but not
where delicate sorts are to grow), mix in a little artificial
manure or a little very old and rotten cow manure, so
old as to have become almost like soil ; or the bulbs may
be planted in six or seven inch pots in the same way.
Plant the bulbs as early as possible in August, almost
touching each other, and covered with half an inch or
more of soil, except the very small bulbs, which require
less. Then pack all the boxes and pots side by side in
some open space on a foundation of ashes. Take care
they stand quite level, and fill up around and between
them with ashes up to their rims or edges and cover
them with about five or six inches of cocoa fibre refuse,
except the small growing kinds, which only need about
three inches. Leave them outside for at least three
months ; the boxes will then be full of roots, and most
of the varieties will have made growth upwards. Now
remove them from outside and place in a cold frame,
again letting them rest on a few inches of ashes, quite
level. Let the young tender growth, which is now
exposed, be shaded from strong light for a few days
until the white shoots turn green, then admit full light.
A space should be left between the boxes or pots and
the sides of the frames, and this and any spaces between
the boxes and pots themselves should be filled in with
ashes ; and about a quarter to half-an-inch of cocoa fibre
may with advantage be strewn over the surface of the
soil in the boxes and pots. Through the winter the
frames should be well protected with mats at night and
during severe frosty days, so as to secure early flowering.
Plenty of air must be admitted, except in severe weather,
for the plants must not be allowed to become drawn.
If afterwards removed to a greenhouse, they must, for
the same reason, be kept near the glass. A most
important point is the watering, which must be regularly

given (except, of course, during frost) after the boxes,
etc., are put in the cold frame.   At first, all that is
necessary is to keep the soil nicely moist; but it should
be remembered that the boxes are full of roots.   When
the plants are making strong growth above ground,
they will need plenty of water in increasing supply until
as flowering time approaches, they get a good watering
three times a week.   In this way remarkably fine
flowers may be obtained.   Do not neglect watering
after the flowers have been cut, or the bulbs will
dwindle and become worthless, but put the boxes, etc.,
outside in the open air, tying up the foliage loosely to
prevent breakage, and give plenty of water until the
leaves turn yellow.   Then plant the bulbs in bed or
border for blooming next season.   The fineness of the
blooms obtained by this method is due to the regular
supplies of water, coupled with perfect drainage, as
well as protection from extremes of cold.

N. TAZETTA.—N. Tazetta, the "Clustered Narcissus"
(Syn. *Polyanthus Narcissus*), has long been naturalised
in the Scilly Isles and Cornwall, but does not lend
itself so readily to outdoor cultivation in England
generally as the less widely diffused solitary—or one
flowered—species and varieties; for it belongs naturally
to a much warmer and more sunny climate than that of
Northern Europe.   And yet the perseverance and skill
of our neighbours the Dutch, through more than three
centuries of cultivation, have made this peculiarly a
Dutch flower, and it is to them that we owe most of the
choicer varieties now in general cultivation.   In growing
Tazettas in England recourse is generally had to
"forcing."   There are also a few varieties of the other
species which it is found useful to force for an early
supply of cut flowers.

FORCING.—The Narcissus dislikes forcing, and this
when necessary must be applied very gently and with

great care, and no bottom heat must be used. The method is as follows:—In August, and successionally in September and October, Tazetta bulbs should be planted in good rich soil with a liberal mixture of coarse silver sand and *thoroughly-rotted* cow manure. One bulb should be put in a five-inch pot, three in a six-inch pot, and six in an eight-inch pot. The other kinds of Daffodils which are good for forcing being most of them smaller, a larger number may be put in the pots. They must then be treated out of doors as recommended above for *cold frames*, and when in due course removed from the plunging material, should be placed in quarters where frost is just excluded, the tender shoots being gradually accustomed to the light, plenty of air being given and the plants not allowed to become drawn. When thoroughly at home in their new surroundings they may be successionally removed to a *moderately warm and moist* temperature, and brought on, as required, for flowering; but any attempt to force them before the flower bud can be seen is undesirable, and the more gently they are forced the better will be the results. Overforcing produces weak, drooping foliage and flowers out of character.

The best varieties of Polyanthus Narcissus are as follows :—

(1) *White perianth, yellow crown.*

DOUBLE ROMAN Narcissus, early, with orange nectaries.

BAZELMAN MAJOR, dark yellow cup.

GLORIOSUS, orange cup.

GRAND MONARCH, citron cup.

HER MAJESTY, deep golden cup.

MÆSTRO, orange cup.

MONT CENIS, early dwarf, rich yellow cup.

QUEEN OF THE NETHERLANDS, rich yellow cup.

STATES GENERAL, citron cup.

D

(2) *White Tazettas.*

PAPER WHITE (grandiflorus), large, pure white.
SCILLY WHITE, early.
WHITE PEARL, pure white.

(3) *Yellow or primrose perianth ; cup yellow or orange.*

ADONIA, deep primrose ; deep orange-yellow cup.
BATHURST, dwarf, primrose ; deep golden cup.
JAUNE SUPRÈME, buff-primrose ; orange-yellow cup.
LORD CANNING, sulphur-yellow ; light orange cup.
SIR ISAAC NEWTON, yellow ; orange cup.
PRESIDENT HARRISON, pale yellow ; rich yellow cup.
GRAND SOLEIL D'OR, golden ; brilliant orange cup.

Northern Chinese Variety.

The SACRED LILY, or "Flower of good luck," called also by the Chinese "Jos-flower" and "Water-fairy." White, with yellow cup.

This variety may also be grown, as described below, with marble chips and water, and then it matures its flowers very rapidly.

OTHER DAFFODILS for forcing are—

Telamonius plenus.	*Golden Spur.*	*Princeps.*
Obvallaris.	*Horsfield.*	*Poeticus Ornatus.*
Ard Righ.	*Victoria.*	*Poeticus Præcox Grandiflorus.*

CULTIVATION IN WATER.—Although the practice is not now very common, Daffodils, especially the trumpet varieties, may be grown like Hyacinths IN GLASS VASES OF WATER. Rain or soft water should be used, if possible. The larger varieties recommended for cultivation in cold frames and those for "forcing" are suitable for this purpose.

Bulbs of the Chinese "Flower of good luck," and of such *Polyanthus* varieties as "Paper White," "Queen of the Netherlands," "Mont Cenis," "Maestro," "Grand

Soleil d'Or," and "Gloriosus," may be grown in any room in which the temperature is moderately warm, IN BOWLS OF WATER, several bulbs in a bowl, marble chips being placed with them to prevent them from floating and keep them in position. The water must be changed frequently (it is better to do this at least every other day), and the bulbs (especially those of the Chinese variety) may be brought very rapidly into bloom.

Both Tazettas and the other kinds already recommended for cold frame cultivation may also be grown IN JARS, without drainage, IN A MIXTURE OF COCOA FIBRE (or moss fibre) AND SHELL SHINGLE (about four parts of the fibre to one of ground shell); coarse silver sand may be substituted, if more convenient, for the shell. Mr Robert Sydenham, of Birmingham, has grown bulbs in this way with great success. The following plan may be adopted as advised by him:—Put small pieces of charcoal about the size of small nuts at the bottom of the jars; then having mixed the fibre and ground shell *very thoroughly* together, add one or two inches of the composition according to the size of the vase; place the bulbs upon it, and fill up nearly to the brim with more of the composition. No vacant spaces must be left at the sides of the vase, but the fibre must be made only moderately firm, not jammed in very tightly. *Great* care should be taken to keep the composition fairly moist (not sodden), fresh water being given as often as necessary, and the surplus water allowed to drain away by turning the jar on its side. Kept at first in any airy cellar or room, not in a confined cupboard, the jars may be brought, when the bulbs have grown about an inch out of the composition, gradually into the light. As much air and light as possible must be given, but of course frost must be guarded against. *The composition must never be allowed to get really dry.* This method is suitable for ladies who have no garden or greenhouse but wish to grow some flowers in the house. The fibre and shell are cleanly to handle, and the jars light to lift. The number of bulbs (which should be put fairly close together) must, of course, be suited to the size of the jar, and small jars should be used for the smaller bulbs.

CHAPTER X.

THE Narcissus grower has not many enemies or plant diseases to contend with. Mice and rabbits leave the bulbs severely alone on account of their poisonous character. The flowers too are practically unmolested. A misguided sparrow, or an inexperienced finch, will sometimes at the beginning of the Daffodil season make a grab at an opening bud, and spoil the flower; but the taste is not to his liking, and he will very soon discontinue the practice. Neither do cattle interfere with the leaves and flowers growing in the meadow grass.

But Narcissus has one deadly enemy—*Merodon equestris*, the Narcissus or Daffodil fly, whose grub attacks the bulb, and, eating into its core, causes decay, and ultimately destroys it. This terrible pest did not trouble the older generation of Daffodil growers in North Europe. Coming originally from the South, it was not until 1840 that it became well-established in Holland, and thence it has been handed on to us in imported bulbs. The rapidity of its increase may be judged by the fact that, during its short life of about two months (beginning in May and lasting sometimes till July), the female fly may lay as many as 100 eggs, one by one, in different places. This enemy has become increasingly tiresome and destructive of late, and it behoves every Narcissus grower to get sufficient knowledge of its appearance and habits to enable him to detect its presence in his garden, and to check its increase, if he cannot wholly exterminate it.

53

A monograph on this subject, published in Haärlem in 1885 by Dr J. Ritzema Bos, is the standard authority, but further investigations have been made more recently. For the present state of our knowledge on the subject, the reader is referred to two most valuable notes, by that well-known horticulturist and Daffodil authority, the Rev. W. Wilks, which appeared in the Journals of the Royal Horticultural Society for 1901 and 1902 (vol. 26, page 249, and vol. 27, page 181). For the benefit of those readers who have not yet secured to themselves the advantages of becoming Fellows of the Royal Horticultural Society, some of the information contained in these notes, and a few extracts from them, are now given.

In general appearance the Narcissus-fly is not unlike a small black " bumble-bee," though, when it settles in the sun, it will often be seen to have brown, yellow, and sometimes red or white markings upon it. It is very hairy, but may be easily distinguished from the " bumble-bee " by its having only two wings, and being narrower in form. It is scarcely half an inch long, and about an inch across the wings when open. It may be distinguished from the common drone-fly by its size; it is distinctly smaller, and also has a stout spine at the tip of the middle joint of the hind leg.

It may be identified in the garden by two well-marked characteristics, which, taken together, make it difficult to mistake. Its manner of flight is most marked, very much like that of the drone-bee or the humming-bird hawk-moth. Mr Wilks says: "they hover over the Daffodil beds, moving their wings so swiftly that they do not seem to work them at all, and, if undisturbed, they will poise themselves thus for three or more minutes at a time, without change of place or position. Then suddenly they dart to right or left (hardly ever, I think, straight forward) with lightning speed, too quickly for

eye to follow them." The other peculiarity is the
noise it makes as it flies about, in this respect quite
unlike the common drone-fly. Mr Wilks says : "I can
only describe it as something between a shriek and a
whistle ; it is of course a small sound in itself, but great

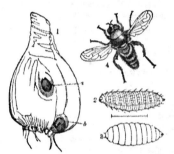

MERODON EQUESTRIS (*The Narcissus Fly*).
with grub ; and an infested bulb with two holes.

1. Neck of the bulb, down which the grub generally makes its
   entrance.
2. The full-grown grub.
3. The chrysalis.
4. The fully developed fly.
a. Hole in shoulder of bulb, probably made by a half-grown grub
   migrating from one bulb to another.
b. Hole made by the grub at the base of the bulb.

(*From Burbidge's "The Narcissus," 1875. By kind permission of the
publishers, Messrs Lovell, Reeve & Co.*)

in comparison to the size of its author, and you can
often hear it at a distance at which the fly itself is
unperceived." When it settles it generally hides
amongst the Daffodil leaves, and if disturbed goes a
very short distance and then settles again. It is in May
and June, and occasionally at the beginning of July, that

the Merodon is to be seen flying about, and it should then be caught, when this is possible, and destroyed. The female fly probably settles amongst the leaves, as near as possible to the top of the bulb, when she is laying her eggs, although some have thought that she drops them as she hovers over the beds. The eggs would seem to hatch quickly, then the little grub at once finds its way into the bulb and begins its destructive work. It used to be thought that entering the neck of the bulb (and growing larger and larger as it went) it gradually ate its way down to the base, and thence, when full grown, quitted the bulb; but this opinion must now be modified, although it may be *sometimes* the method of procedure. An opinion has been mooted that the little grub passes down outside the bulb, and enters it from the base, making its way upwards, and leaving the bulb near the top. Mr Percy Williams, of Lanarth, Cornwall, a well-known Daffodil grower, has made some experiments with a view to settling this point, and, after much careful examination, is of opinion that the latter method is the grub's usual course of action. Last autumn, as a further experiment, he selected a dozen bulbs, which seemed to be quite free from disease except that they showed a *very small* black spot on the base about the size of a small pin's head, and these, after being grown in pots in a cold greenhouse, were examined by the Narcissus Committee of the Royal Horticultural Society. Eleven out of the twelve were found to have *Merodon* grubs in them. Mr Williams' experiments seem to prove that *sometimes* the grubs may enter at the base, but are not decisive as to its general habit. The most probable opinion would seem to be that of Mr Wilks, which he thus expresses, "from my own observation I am convinced that, in the majority of cases, if not in all, the grubs work their way down through the neck of the bulb, and eat their way straight

down the very centre of the heart of the bulb to the
base, where they seem *generally* to make a small hole
through, possibly to act as a cloaca, and then they turn
upwards to finish their course, emerging again by the
same road [almost exactly at the spot where] they
entered. I have found young grubs embedded in the
centre of the bulb-neck, and on cutting open the bulbs
they have been as yet perfectly sound." Sometimes two
holes will be observed in the infested bulb, one at the
base, and one higher up. As to this, Mr Wilks says,
"in the case of two distinct holes, I believe the one in
the shoulder generally has been made by a half-grown
grub migrating to a new home and boring its way in;
it then bores on to make its sewage-hole at the base,
and, having done this, fattens itself up upon the substance of the bulb." After leaving the bulb, the grub
buries itself in the surrounding earth, becomes trans-
formed into a chrysalis, and so remains until the following spring, when the flies issue forth about the month
of May. The grubs are smooth and oval in shape, of
a yellowish-white colour, and, when full grown, about
half an inch long; and the chrysalis is much wrinkled,
and very much resembles the grub in appearance.

When the harvested bulbs are found to have such
holes as have been spoken of it is a sufficient intimation
of their being infested by the Narcissus grub, but these
holes are not always to be seen until a later date than
the proper time for planting the bulbs. If, however,
the necks of apparently sound bulbs, when pinched, feel
soft and spongy mischief should be suspected, and an
examination made, and all infested bulbs destroyed; there
is no method of killing the grubs within, which will not
also destroy the bulb. Such careful hand-picking of the
bulbs during the first three weeks of August will tend
greatly to diminish the pest, and many of the flies may
be caught and killed in May and June with a butterfly-

net; they are not easy to catch when on the wing, but may be captured without much difficulty when they settle. A Dutch authority, Mr A. C. Groenewegen, advises to search for the chrysalides and remove them from the soil just before the plants flower, as at that time they are found near the surface of the ground, and this method is said to have proved very successful. A suggestion has also been made, which may perhaps be worth adopting, that plates of treacle, with the edges smeared with honey to attract the fly, should be placed about the beds as a trap to catch them.

The Narcissus, on the whole, is very robust in health. The chief cause of loss among some of the more tender varieties is an insidious form of disease which goes by the name of basal-rot. It shows itself most often among the White-trumpet Daffodils, but also does a good deal of mischief among some of the more delicate of the Self-Yellows. The Medio-coronati and Parvi-coronati sections suffer in a much less degree, but it often affects the Leedsii group and Jonquilla and the Tazettas. The symptoms of this disease as seen above ground are a premature growth of the flower stalk, "which produces only stunted and badly shaped flowers," and the unhealthy and dwarfed condition of the leaves; underground the base of the bulb becomes soft, its coats discoloured, and the spaces between them wet and offensive, and there is a total failure of power in the disc round the base, to produce the necessary growth of new root. The bulb becomes flabby, decays and dies. It is not generally worth the time and trouble incurred in trying to cure such diseased bulbs, though, when *valuable*, they may, if taken in time, be transplanted into dry soil in a well raised bed, or planted out in grass, with some possibility of a cure. The White Daffodils, when under suitable conditions and doing well, are better for not being moved too often, but in situations where they suffer much from this disease they will be benefited by annual lifting and replanting. It is in cold and wet soils and seasons, and also in soils that are highly manured, that basal-rot will be found most prevalent. The best *general* precaution against it is to adhere to sound rules of cultivation.

Some mischief is occasionally done by what is called black-canker. This is ascribed by some authorities to Peziza cibovioides, but the damage done is not considerable. A good general rule for keeping the stock in first-rate condition is to carefully examine the bulbs when first taken out of the ground, and to discard those in which any appreciable portion of the ring of roots round the base is not in a thoroughly healthy condition.

CHAPTER XI.

THE flowers we admire so much in a good daffodil garden, or at a Daffodil Show, are some of them true species, *e.g.* Poeticus, Jonquilla, Triandrus, Juncifolius, Pseudo-Narcissus, etc., etc., and some of them wild hybrids, though now cultivated in gardens, *e.g.* Odorus, Bernardi, etc., etc., but the greater number are "garden hybrids," and other garden seedlings, the result of cross-fertilisation, either natural or artificial, which has been effected between different daffodils under cultivation. Cross-fertilisation is therefore a very important matter in daffodil culture.

Within the perianth tube and corona of every daffodil flower, as was pointed out in chapter ii., there is a long slender style ; this is flattened out at the end into what is called the "stigma"; and lying round it are six stamens with enlargements at the ends called "anthers." When fully developed the anthers are covered with a very fine dust-like substance called "pollen," and the stigma at its full development exhibits a slight stickiness which assists it in retaining any pollen dust that may be brought in contact with it. Such contact may be effected in the course of nature by the action of the wind or by insects who carry the pollen on their bodies, and when this "*pollination*" takes place under favourable conditions, the flower becomes fertilised, and the ovary which is connected with the style and stigma is enabled to produce fruitful seeds ; and these seeds, when properly

60

MEDIO-CORONATI

(*An Incomparabilis form*)

N. PSEUDO-NARCISSUS × N. POETICUS

ripened and sown, in due course produce fresh plants. The application of the pollen of one flower to the stigma of another individual is called *cross-pollination*, and the fertilisation consequent upon it is *cross-fertilisation.*

When in a natural habitat where the Narcissus has been established for centuries a flower is either self-fertilised or fertilised by pollen from another similar to itself it may be expected to reproduce its own character-istics in its offspring. But when the pollen is from a flower of another species, or of a quite distinct type, the offspring will be found to be intermediate between the two parents, though in such cases seeds from the same seed-pod will generally produce flowers differing much from each other—reproducing in different degrees of resemblance the peculiar characteristics of their parents.

But cross-fertilisation may be effected artificially by the hand of man, as well as naturally by wind or insect. And seeds of naturally fertilised flowers may be collected and sown, and a selection made of good new varieties resulting from them. The earliest mention of Narcissus seedling raising would seem to be that by Theophrastus of Eresus (B.C. 374-285). But it is only of compara-tively late years—since Dean Herbert began both to practise this important work and to urge it upon others —that artificial cross-fertilisation and seedling raising have been carried on *on a large scale* and with such magnificent results as we are now enjoying. Most of the fine standard named varieties of garden hybrids, which make the choice daffodil gardens of to-day so much richer and more beautiful than were those of Parkinson and the old gardeners, are the result of the labours of the daffodil enthusiasts of the last half century, especi-ally of Mr W. Backhouse, of St John's, Walsingham, Mr Leeds, of Longford Bridge, Manchester, and in a less degree the Rev. Mr Nelson, of Aldborough, and

Mr Horsfield, the Lancashire weaver. And still more beautiful forms, and in still greater abundance, are being yearly brought into existence by the numerous seedling raisers of our own time. The Rev. G. H. Engleheart has made this branch of work peculiarly his own, has attained a far greater measure of success than any seedling raiser before him, and is being successfully followed, though still at a considerable distance, by many others. Indeed, we can hardly doubt that the beautiful new flowers associated with his name and with those of Barr, Wilmott, Williams, De Graaff, Kendall, R. O. Backhouse and others, will soon make a large proportion of our existing standard varieties quite obsolete.

The work then of cross-fertilisation and seedling raising is full of encouragement, and for those who have enough spare time to devote to it a continual source of interest and pleasure ; and where there is a little garden or greenhouse space at disposal and a few good varieties to work upon, the amateur gardener will be wise to act upon Mr Burbidge's wholesome advice—" raise seedlings —hybrids if you can—but raise seedlings."

How to do it.—Cross-fertilisation should be effected on bright sunny mornings. All the equipment absolutely necessary is a small camel's-hair brush. With this, slightly moistened with water, the pollen is removed from the anthers of one flower and placed upon the stigma of any other which is thought to be suitable for crossing with it.

As soon as this has been done a piece of coloured thread or scarlet wool should be tied round the flower-stalk as a mark that it has been operated upon, and to save the flower from being cut for use in the house ; and a record should be made in a note-book of the pollen used in each separate case. The stalk should be tied up to prevent any accidental breakage, and the seed-pod watched, as it swells, so that it may be gathered before it is quite ready to burst; otherwise the seeds may be lost.

Very desirable precautions are—to cut out the anthers of the proposed seed-bearing flower while in a young state and so prevent possible self-fertilisation, which in some varieties very rapidly takes place, and also to protect it from wind or insect-carried pollen with glass or fine muslin. And it is much easier to ensure success in making the desired cross when the mother plants are grown in pots in a greenhouse.

The seeds should be sown as soon as ripe, in boxes (or pots and pans), and kept in a cold frame plunged in cocoa-fibre on a well-drained and level bottom. The soil in which they are sown should have a good mixture of sharp sand, and good drainage should be supplied by a layer of rough, half-rotten turf. The seeds should be covered with about half an inch, or a little less, of sandy soil; the little bulbs when produced have a remarkable way of their own of working down to their proper depth. The young plants do not come up all at once but at intervals throughout the winter, and their tender, narrow, rush-like leaves must be duly protected from snails and slugs.

The young plants should be kept in their boxes, pots or pans, in the cold frame for their first two years, and afterwards planted out in the open in beds raised slightly above the surrounding level.

Seeds from the very small growing kinds, such as Triandrus, Juncifolius, and Cyclamineus, generally flower in the third year after sowing, and a good many seeds of other kinds may be expected to show flower the fourth year; but five years is the usual time for the large growing kinds, and even then they do not exhibit their true character at once, but may go on improving for several years. This seems a long time to wait for results; but if an *annual* sowing is made, when once the first three or four years are over, new varieties may be looked for and enjoyed every year.

Note that secondary crosses may be effected—such as those between Poeticus and Incomparabilis (which is itself a cross between *Poeticus* and Pseudo-Narcissus)— and may be expected to give additional brilliancy to the scarlet or orange colouring in the offspring.

Such a large subject as that of the raising of new varieties can only be lightly touched upon in a handbook such as this, but one hint of great importance may be added to what has been already said. In selecting the varieties on which cross-fertilisation is to be practised, only those flowers which are of particularly fine form and of good substance in the perianth segments should be chosen, or at least one of the parents should have a very substantial perianth. Now that we have so large and so rapidly increasing a number of handsome red-cups, the efforts of hybridisers should be directed to obtain what is far less common as yet in this class of flowers, viz., a really good, substantial, well-shaped perianth. We do not want so many of those red-cupped flowers that only look well at a little distance, or when massed together in a bunch; a brilliant cup is an excellent thing, but it is not enough unless associated with a perianth which bears examining, critically and closely.

Efforts should also be made by seed sowing and selection to obtain White Trumpets and early Self-Yellow Trumpet Daffodils of better constitution than those we now have.

CHAPTER XII.

IT is by no means an easy task out of the almost endless varieties now in cultivation to make a good selection, and the beginner certainly needs guidance. (1) Regard should be had to the relative time of flowering of the different kinds, so as to secure a long flowering season; (2) the collection should be representative of all the more beautiful classes; (3) where several varieties which flower together are rather similar, the inferior should be dispensed with; (4) a first-rate collection should have a considerable proportion of the beautiful white and sulphur Daffodils, and of the white *Leedsii* Narcissi, and also a good number of the red-cupped varieties. All this cannot be effected *at once* without considerable expense and without considerable knowledge. But with well-chosen lists to select from it may be accomplished gradually, and the expense kept within reasonable limits.

It is a great but very common mistake to spend money in buying poor varieties because they are cheap. Good things take no more space and give, as a rule, no more trouble than poor ones; and with the Narcissus, as with most other things, "the best are the cheapest" in the long run. Many of the best are costly, but some most excellent kinds may be bought at a very reasonable price. I would suggest that about half the initial outlay should be invested in varieties which are both cheap and, at the same time, of high quality : these will

E   65 at once give a good supply of fine flowers. The other half should be spent in a smaller number of the more expensive kinds: these latter will gradually increase and build up a fine collection. Begin chiefly with the vigorous sorts, and as you gain experience in cultivation add the more delicate and uncertain varieties.

With a view to assisting beginners in this process, I have prepared five lists which contain among them under different heads most of the best varieties at present in commerce. Lists A, B and C contain kinds which are easily grown, and they are progressive in the matter of expense. List D contains very beautiful kinds indispensable to a fine collection, but of delicate or uncertain constitution. List E is to a large extent a list for the future rather than for the present. It comprises a number of exceedingly fine varieties from among the newer seedlings, many of which are not yet in commerce, the others being still scarce and most of them very expensive. They are all of them well worth purchasing, when they can be obtained, and will almost certainly in the course of time supersede a number of the standard varieties which are now highly valued. In the first four lists numbers from one to six are added in brackets after each name to show roughly the relative time of flowering. I think they will be found fairly correct and a useful guide.

THE FIVE LISTS.

A.—Thirty-seven cheap and very good varieties of which only a very few are at all uncertain in constitution.

DAFFODILS.

Golden Spur.—A large flower of deep rich self-yellow and beautiful form, very early; of rather uncertain constitution ; should be grown without manure in fibrous maiden loam (1).

Emperor.—A large, stately, self-yellow flower (3).

P. R. Barr.—Very similar to " Emperor," but a little later; is smaller and more refined in form (4).

Bicolor *Princeps.*—One of the earliest bicolors; very useful. It is also a very good subject for cold frame treatment (1).

Bicolor *Horsfield*, or Bicolor *Empress.*—These are very similar. Horsfield when well-grown makes rather larger flowers, is about a week earlier than " Empress," and is rather more graceful in form, but the flower of " Empress " has more substance and lasts longer (2).

Bicolor " *Grandee.*"—Flowers in succession to " Horsfield " and " Empress," to which it is similar. It has very finely shaped perianth segments. Late and very fine (5).

Sulphur Ajax *W. P. Milner.*—A dwarf sulphur-coloured Daffodil changing to white; valuable both for its elegance and its good constitution (3).

STAR NARCISSI.

Incomparabilis *Queen Bess.*—The earliest of the Star Narcissi (1).

Incomparabilis *Sir Watkin.*—A gigantic light yellow flower; a little coarse in form, but very showy and invaluable for decorative purposes (2).

Incomparabilis *Gwyther.*—Yellow with orange-stained cup (3).

Incomparabilis *Autocrat* and Incomparabilis *Frank Miles.* —Two remarkably fine forms of self-yellow Incomparables, quite distinct from each other (3).

Incomparabilis *Stella Superba* (3).—See CERTIFICATED VARIETIES, page 91.

Incomparabilis *Beauty* (3). — See CERTIFICATED

VARIETIES, page 81.
Incomparabilis *Semi-partitus*.—Of a soft primrose shade, very charming and distinct in form and colour (4).
Incomparabilis *King of the Netherlands*.—A strong-growing, showy, rather late flower (4).
Double Incomparabilis *Golden Phœnix* ("Butter and Eggs").—Large double rose-shaped flowers, yellow with orange coronal segments (3).
Double Incomparabilis *Orange Phœnix* ("Eggs and Bacon").—Large double rose-shaped flowers, white with reddish-orange coronal segments (3).
Double Incomparabilis *Sulphur Phœnix* ("Codlins and Cream").—White and sulphur mingled; the most beautiful of the double Narcissi (4).
Barrii *Orphée*.—The earliest of the beautiful Barrii section (3).
Barrii *Maurice Vilmorin*.—Creamy white, with long cup heavily stained orange-scarlet; dwarf, lovely (3).
Barrii *Flora Wilson*.—White with bright red edge to cup; very pretty. It is better not to gather the buds of this particular variety until the flower is quite expanded (4).
Barrii *Conspicuus* (4).—See CERTIFICATED VARIETIES, page 82.
Leedsii *Minnie Hume*.—A most lovely flower; the lemon-coloured cup changes gradually to pure white (3).
Leedsii *Mrs Langtry*. — White with bright canary edge to cup (4).
Leedsii *Mary Magdalen de Graaff*.—A beautiful form with very striking and distinct red colouring in cup. Is usually two flowered (4).
Nelsoni *Mrs Backhouse*.—A more finely shaped and more lasting flower than the better known "Nelsoni Major" (4).
Odorus *Rugulosus*.—Has small very rich yellow flowers

MEDIO-CORONATI
(*A Leedsii form*)
NARCISSUS "MRS. LANGTRY"

(several on a stem), and rush-like foliage. Better than "Odorus Campernelli" (2).

Macleaii.—Very small flowers. White with yellow cylindrical cup. Very distinct and pretty (4).

TRUE NARCISSI.

Burbidgei *John Bain.*—The earliest of the Burbidgei varieties; a handsome flower (3).

Burbidgei *Baroness Heath.*—Very distinct; yellow, with orange-scarlet cup (3).

Burbidgei *Falstaff* (4), or Burbidgei *Ellen Barr* (4). —Two very lovely, well-formed and not very dissimilar flowers; white with orange-stained crown. If only one of the two is grown it should be "Falstaff."

Burbidgei *Vanessa.*—Rather late; of a striking shade of pale yellow and perfect shape (4).

Poeticus *Præcox grandiflorus.*—Rather earlier than "Ornatus," and quite distinct in form (4).

Poeticus *Ornatus.*—An early and very fine form of the Pheasant's Eye group (4). Probably of Italian origin.

Poeticus *Poetarum.*—A little later than "Ornatus," and with the red in the crown more widely diffused (5).

Poeticus of Gardens. — The beautiful late-flowering "Pheasant's Eye" (6).

Double Poeticus.—With pure white "Gardenia flowered" blossoms; very late; requires a moist situation, rather strong loam, and not to stand more than two years in one place (6).

LIST B.

Nineteen rather more expensive, very fine.

DAFFODILS.

Bicolor *Mrs Walter Ware.*—Not very large, but about the finest in form of all the Bicolors (3).

Bicolor *Victoria* (3).—See Certificated Varieties, page 92.

Bicolor *J. B. M. Camm* (3).—See Certificated Varieties, page 86.

Star Narcissi.

Incomparabilis *C. J. Backhouse* (3).—See Certificated Varieties, page 82.

Incomparabilis *Splendens.*—Sulphur with large red-edged cup (3).

Incomparabilis *Princess Mary* (3).—See Certificated Varieties, page 89.

Incomparabilis *Mabel Cowan.*—Fine, rather late, with red-margined cup (4).

Barrii *Crown Prince.*—One of the very best; rather late flowering, white with red-stained cup (4).

Barrii •*Mrs Bowley.*—White with striking red cup; distinct and beautiful (4).

Leedsii *Grand Duchess.*—One of the earliest of the Leedsii group; white with orange-stained cup (3).

Leedsii *Gem.*—An elegant, drooping, bell-shaped white flower; very distinct (3).

Leedsii *Madge Matthew.*—A very elegant white flower, rather early; very distinct.

Leedsii *Beatrice.*—Pure white, of very elegant form (4).

Leedsii *Duchess of Westminster.*—One of the very best (4). See Certificated Varieties, page 83.

Leedsii *Katherine Spurrell.*—Another of the best; with broad over-lapping perianth; striking dark green eye to the cup (4).

True Narcissi.

Burbidgei *Model.*—Of remarkably fine form; white, with orange-stained cup (4).

Burbidgei *Princess Louise.*—The orange-red of the cup passes off apricot, giving the flower a very lovely appearance (4).

Burbidgei *Beatrice Heseltine.* — One of the latest and one of the best of the Burbidgei group; most valuable for its fine form and beautiful red-edged cup as well as for its lateness (5).

Poeticus *Almira.*—Very fine rounded white perianth, cup margined deep red. One of the best of the new Poeticus section (5).

LIST C.

Seventeen still more expensive varieties — most excellent.

DAFFODILS.

Glory of Leiden (3).—See CERTIFICATED VARIETIES, page 85.

Bicolor *Madame Plemp.*—Resembles a huge "Horsfield"; very fine trumpet; a very good doer (3).

White Ajax *Madame de Graaff* (4).—See CERTIFICATED VARIETIES, page 87.

STAR NARCISSI.

Incomparabilis *Queen Sophia* (3).—See CERTIFICATED VARIETIES, page 90.

Incomparabilis *Topaz.*—White perianth; long cup of glowing orange-red.

Incomparabilis *Artemis.*—One of the earlier blooming Incomparables. Fine broad pearly white perianth segments; shallow, well-expanded cup of clear yellow (2).

Incomparabilis *Dorothy York.*—Preferred by some to "Lulworth," but in my opinion "Lulworth" is the more refined and beautiful flower. Probably the red in the cup of "Dorothy York" is more reliable in bad seasons (3).

Incomparabilis *Lulworth* (4). — See CERTIFICATED VARIETIES, page 87.

Incomparabilis *White Wings* (4), see CERTIFICATED VARIETIES, page 93; or Incomp. *Perfectus*; or Incomp. *Louise.*—The two latter are very similar to each other and not very dissimilar from " White Wings," for which if its price be thought too expensive they make very fair substitutes.

Incomparabilis *Gloria Mundi* (4).—See CERTIFICATED VARIETIES, page 84.

Barrii *Doris.*—Considered an improvement on the beautiful Barrii " Maurice Vilmorin " (3).

Barrii *Cecily Hill.*—A fine firm pale yellow flower, with cup stained orange-red; a late flowerer (5).

Barrii *Dorothy Wemyss* (5).—A very fine late flower.— See CERTIFICATED VARIETIES, page 83.

Nelsoni *Aurantius* (4).—See CERTIFICATED VARIETIES. page 80.

Bernardi *H. E. Buxton.*—A rather small but exceedingly beautiful flower. White perianth, brilliant orange-red cup. Like so many of the red cups, the colouring is sometimes (in bad seasons) more or less deficient (5).

Tridymus " Cloth of Gold."—The finest of the Tridymus flowers, about three golden flowers on a tall stem (4).

TRUE NARCISSI.

Poeticus *Dante.*—One of the new Poeticus section. Fine rounded, broad perianth segments, with large eye, deeply suffused red (4).

LIST D.

Twenty-four very fine varieties, necessary to a first-rate collection, which are more or less delicate, or require special treatment. Most of them do best in gritty maiden loam.

DAFFODILS.

Minor.—A very small, early, and elegantly formed self-yellow Daffodil; much better than *Nanus*; to be seen at its best, should be grown in a cold frame (1).

Henry Irving.—A large, very early, self-yellow; should be grown in fibrous maiden loam without manure (1).— See CERTIFICATED VARIETIES, page 85.

Obvallaris (The Tenby Daffodil).—Very early, distinct and fine; medium-sized, self-yellow. Especially good in a cold frame (1).

Capax plenus (Eystettensis).—Very beautiful lemon-coloured double flower, unique in form, the single type of which is not known. Requires warm sandy soil or pot culture (1).

Coronatus (2).—See CERTIFICATED VARIETIES, page 82.

Maximus. — Deep golden self-yellow; the most elegant in form and richest in colour of all the Daffodils (2). Prefers deep planting.

Johnstoni, Queen of Spain (with straight trumpet) or *King of Spain* (with trumpet spreading at mouth).— Light self-yellow, with reflexed perianth, very distinct, and among the most beautiful; are best in a cold frame (3).

Captain Nelson (3).—See CERTIFICATED VARIETIES, page 81.

John Nelson. — Another fine distinct, rather late flowering yellow daffodil (3).

Bicolor *Ione.*—Fine dwarf-growing Bicolor, with elegant, imbricated, hooded bloom; raised by Mr W. B. Hartland of Cork.

Sulphur Ajax *Pallidus præcox.* A lovely but very delicate flower (1).—See CERTIFICATED VARIETIES, page 89.

White Ajax *Mrs Thompson.*—An early white Daffodil

(the pale lemon trumpet passes off white); has a less uncertain constitution than many others of the same group (2).

White Ajax *Cernuus* (1), or *Tortuosus* (2).—Very elegant white Daffodils. The former is rather earlier, and perhaps more elegant.

White Ajax *Albicans.*—Less delicate than most of the white Daffodils (2).

White Ajax *Cernuus pulcher.*—A very distinct white Daffodil, with twisted, drooping perianth segments; of good constitution (2).

White Ajax *Mrs Burbidge.*—A very fine white Daffodil, one of the best (2).

White Ajax *Mrs Camm.*—Rather late flowering (4). See CERTIFICATED VARIETIES, page 88.

White Ajax *Mrs Vincent.*—A very distinct and perfect white flower; late (4).

White Ajax *Matson Vincent.*—A small, very pretty, pure white flower, with fine trumpet (4).

STAR NARCISSI.

Triandrus albus (" Angel's Tears ").—An elegant white drooping flower, with reflexed perianth ; is best grown in pans in a cold frame (3).

Calathinus (3). — See CERTIFICATED VARIETIES, page 81.

Juncifolius.—The smallest Narcissus; is best grown in pans in a cold frame (4).—See CERTIFICATED VARIETIES, page 86.

TRUE NARCISSI.

Tenuior.—The slender straw-coloured Narcissus has several flowers on a stem; very elegant ; is best grown in a cold frame (4).

Intermedius Bifrons " *Sunset.*"—A very beautiful small

Tazetta, which, in most seasons, does well in the border, and is always excellent in a cold frame (4).—See CERTIFICATED VARIETIES, page 91.

LIST E.

A list chiefly for the future. Flowers of the very highest excellence, some of which are not yet in commerce, and others still very expensive: but all of them most desirable.

DAFFODILS.

Yellow Ajax.

Golden Bell. See p. 85.	Herald, p. 95.	Van Waveren's Giant, p. 92.
Glory of Noordwyk, p. 85.	King Alfred, p. 86.	
	Lord Roberts, p. 87.	
	Monarch, p. 96.	

Bicolor Ajax.

Celia, p. 94.	Mrs Morland Cros-	Weardale Perfection,
Coronet, p. 94.	field, p. 96.	p. 92.
Duke of Bedford, p. 83.	Norma, p. 96,	Wilhelmina, p. 93.
Ellen Willmott, p. 84.	Queen Christina,	
Jeannie Woodhouse, p. 95.	p. 90.	

White and Sulphur Ajax.

Florence, p. 84.	Peter Barr, p. 89.	Warley Magna, p. 92.
Genoa, p. 95.	St Cecilia, p. 91.	

Johnstoni.

Ada, p. 79.	Dorothy Kingsmill, p. 83.	Moonray, p. 88.
Betty Berkeley, p. 81.		Snowdrop, p. 91.
Cecil Rhodes, p. 81.	Eleanor Berkeley,	
Countess Grey, p. 82.	p. 84.	

STAR NARCISSI.

Incomparabilis.

Diana, p. 83.
Electra, p. 95.
Firebrand, p. 95.
Flambeau, p. 84.
Flamingo, p. 95.
Lady Margaret Bos-cawen, p. 87.

Lady Watkin, p. 95.
Lucifer, p. 87.
Mrs Berkeley, p. 88.
Ptarmigan, p. 96.
Queen Alexandra, p. 89.

Robert Berkeley, p. 90.
Sea Bird, p. 90.
Solfatare, p. 96.
Warden, p. 96.
Will Scarlett, p. 93.

Double Incomparabilis.

Primrose Phœnix, p. 89.

Leedsii.

Ariadne, p. 94.
Bridal flower, p. 94.
Elaine, p. 84.

Enid, p. 95.
Lilian, p. 96.
Moonbeam, p. 88.

Water-witch, p. 96.
White Lady, p. 92.
White Queen, p. 93.

Bernardi.

Philip Hurt, p. 89.

TRUE NARCISSI.

Burbidgei.

Albatross, p. 79.
Astrardente, p. 94.
Bullfinch, p. 94.
Blood Orange, p. 94.
Cresset, p. 82.

Egret, p. 94.
Imogen, p. 95.
Incognita, p. 86.
Occident, p. 96.
Oriflamme, p. 89.

Sceptre, p. 96.
Sea Gull, p. 96.
Southern Star, p. 91.
Watchfire, p. 92.

Poeticus.

Cassandra, p. 81.
Chaucer, p. 94.
Epic, p. 95.
Glory, p. 95.

Herrick, p. 85.
Homer, p. 85.
Horace, p. 95.
Laura, p. 95.

Laureate, p. 95.
Virgil, p. 92.

MAGNI-CORONATI

(*A Pseudo-Narcissus form*)

WHITE AJAX "PETER BARR"

CHAPTER XIII.

ANY enthusiastic flower-lover who has been wise enough to become a Fellow of that good old corporation, the Royal Horticultural Society, will know by experience how much help is to be gained (whatever his particular hobby may be) by such membership, both through the opportunities the Society affords of examining new plants and flowers at its fortnightly meetings, by the information given in its most valuable "Journal," and by the labours of its Committees, not to mention the other privileges of its Fellows.

The Daffodil grower is no exception to the rule, and he needs such help at least as much as any other kind of flower-lover. For the number of new and beautiful varieties which have been introduced since the Daffodil Conference in 1884 is so bewildering, and the consequent need of a reliable guide so great, that the fostering and directing hand of the old Society is nowhere perhaps more necessary than in connection with Daffodil culture.

It is through its Narcissus Committee that much of the needed assistance is given. The Narcissus Committee has passed through various phases and performed various functions, but its chief work at the present time seems to be to give information as to any Daffodils which may be sent to it for identification or other advice, and to help the public further, in a more general but very important manner, by distinguishing, through the certificates it grants, particularly meritorious varieties presented at its meetings.

77

A "Book of the Daffodil" would hardly be complete
without a list of those Daffodils which have been certificated by the Royal Horticultural Society. That which
is now given is brought up to date and some short
descriptive particulars in each case added.

In studying this list it must be remembered that an
A.M. (Award of Merit) is *a distinction of great value*, and
even more so of late years than it was some little time
back. It can hardly be doubted that many flowers
marked A.M. during the last year or two would have
received the F.C.C. (First Class Certificate) a few years
ago. The continually increasing number of very high-
class seedlings now raised has brought to the Narcissus
Committee an increasing sense of responsibility to the
public in the matter of Certificates and Awards, and of
the need of increased caution in granting them. The
Committee can only meet fortnightly, but new seedling
flowers are opening out *daily* during a season of about
two months, so that the candidates for honours cannot
be all presented together for examination and award,
and compared side by side. When a flower is presented
which is not only of high excellence, but has also very
distinct features which evidently separate it off from other
Daffodils of its particular group already in cultivation,
it is easy enough for the Committee to award it the
F.C.C. ; but there are many very fine types of flower of
which a great number of very high class seedlings are
raised, and which yet are not so widely different from
each other that this or that particular flower can be with
certainty pronounced so distinctly and so much in advance
of the others not present for comparison as to entitle it
immediately to the F.C.C. The only satisfactory method
in such cases seems to be to mark it off as distinctly and
considerably in advance of the general run of flowers of
its class by giving it an A.M., and leaving it for time and
further experience to prove whether it is so pre-eminent

as to entitle it to the F.C.C. But A.M. as given by the Narcissus Committee may be accepted by the public as a mark that the flower is *of very great excellence.*

List of Narcissi Certificated by the R.H.S.

(F.C.C. = First Class Certificate. A.M. = Award of Merit. B.C. = Botanical Certificate.)

The name in brackets immediately after each variety is that of the grower who presented it to the committee for certificate, and who is not in all cases the actual raiser of the variety.

The group named JOHNSTONI is explained on pp. 13, 14. In the following lists an * after the group-name Burbidgei means that the variety thus specially marked is the result of *Princess Mary* × *a Poeticus seedling,* a cross which has been very fruitful of fine red-cupped varieties.

Ada *(Willmott).*—May 6, 1902. F.C.C. JOHNSTONI. Generally two flowered. White perianth of waxen texture; very pale lemon trumpet.

Aftermath *(Engleheart).*—May 7, 1901. A.M. INCOMPARABILIS. Large flat bloom. Perianth creamy-white, broad and long; cup edged fiery red. Late flowering.

Agnes Harvey *(Spurrell).*—May 20, 1902. A.M. LEEDSII. Said to have Triandrus blood. Late flowering. Perianth pure white; cup with open mouth, pure white, large, solid and globular.

Albatross *(Engleheart).*—April 10, 1894. F.C.C. Probably BURBIDGEI (being probably *P. Ornatus* × *Incomp.*) though originally certificated as a Poeticus. Fine flower, with large and broad white perianth; the cup is a very pale citron, with a ribbon edge of bright orange-scarlet.

Albidus expansus Incomparabilis. See Bianca.

Allen's Beauty (*Willmott*).—April 9, 1901.   A.M.
BICOLOR AJAX.   One of the earliest.   Selected
from wild Pyrenean *Variiformis* by Mr James
Allen, of Shepton Mallet.

Alma (*Engleheart*).—April 10, 1900.   A.M.   SELF-
YELLOW AJAX.   Remarkable chiefly for its
peculiar and rare shade of citron-yellow.

Amber (*Engleheart*).—May 7, 1901.   A.M.   NEL-
SONI ("Empress" × P. Ornatus).   In way of old
Nelsoni Major, but with much broader and flatter
perianth segments.   The long cylindrical crown
is in some seasons flushed with a very beautiful
amber tint.

Apricot (*Barr*).—April 12, 1898.   A.M.   AJAX
(generally classed under *White or Sulphur-coloured*
Daffodils).   Narrow cream-white perianth segments; the long, narrow and straight trumpet
opens primrose and turns a kind of apricot-buff.
It is chiefly remarkable for its new and rather
peculiar colouring.

Aurantius (*Ware*).—April 27, 1886.   F.C.C.   NELSONI.
A very distinct and fine flower.   The best shaped
flower of this class.   The white perianth is broad
and flat, and does not "spider" like Nelsoni
Major.   The clear yellow cup is well expanded
and ribbed, and in favourable seasons suffused
with glowing orange-red.   Must probably be
still ranked as the best Nelsoni.

Aureo-tinctus Leedsi (*Barr*). — March 19, 1878.
F.C.C.   INCOMPARABILIS.   One of the earlier red-
cupped Incomparables.   It is now superseded
by the much finer red cups which have suc-
ceeded it.

Beacon (*Engleheart*).—April 13, 1897.   F.C.C.   BUR-
BIDGEI.   Flat, stiff, sulphur-white segments; flat
crown of fiery, and unusually deep, red.

MAGNI-CORONATI
(*A Johnstoni form*)
NARCISSUS "BETTY BERKELEY"

Beauty (*Barr*).—April 13, 1897. A.M. INCOMPAR-
ABILIS. Tall, handsome flower. Perianth segments sulphur-yellow, with slight yellow bar
down the centre ; large cup, margined orange-
red.

Betty Berkeley (*Willmott*). — April 22, 1902. A.M.
JOHNSTONI. A rather small, very pretty flower of
the " Snowdrop " class. The perianth segments
have a green streak down the back. The trumpet
is never quite white. A dwarfer grower than
" Snowdrop."

Bianca (" Albidus expansus ") (*Barr*).—April 22, 1879.
F.C.C. INCOMP. One of Backhouse's seedlings,
now superseded.

Brigadier (*Engleheart*).—April 18, 1899. A.M. INCOMP.
In the way of a bicolor " Sir Watkin," but of
superior form and finish. Flat-set white perianth,
large open crown of deep yellow ; free in bloom
and increase.

Bulbocodium citrinum (*Ware*). — March 9, 1886.
F.C.C. CORBULARIA. The large sulphur hoop-
petticoat Daffodil.

Calathinus (*Blanchard*).—April 4, 1877. B.C. TRIAN-
DRUS. Most beautiful form. Much larger and
whiter than *Triandrus Albus* and quite distinct.

Campernelle, double (*W. Mauger*).—April 10, 1900.
A.M. ODORUS. The true and very rare form of
Double Campernelle.

Captain Nelson (*Barr, and Ware*).—May 10, 1887.
F.C.C. SELF-YELLOW AJAX. Very large, handsome Daffodil of clear light-yellow with very
fine trumpet.

Cassandra (*Engleheart*).—April 16, 1899. A.M. POETI-
CUS. Tall grower. Perianth very wide and
white ; cup deeply rimmed dark-red.

Cecil Rhodes (*Willmott*). — May 6, 1902. A.M.

F

JOHNSTONI.   Very pale lemon flower.   Well
formed trumpet.   Probably an improvement on
" *Earl Grey.*"

Chancellor (*Engleheart*). — April 24, 1900.   A.M.
NELSONI-INCOMP.   In way of " *Lady Margaret
Boscawen*," but smaller and more Nelsoni-like.
Flat, imbricated, circular segments ivory-white ;
corona short, rather open and rich yellow.

C. J. Backhouse (*Barr*).—April 27, 1886.   F.C.C.
INCOMP.   Yellow; with very striking cup,
wholly red.   There seem to be two " strains " of
this variety, one much better than the other.

Comet (*R. O. Backhouse*).—March 27, 1900.   A.M.
YELLOW AJAX.   Between *Cyclamineus* and
Obvallaris.

Conspicuus (*Barr*).—April 13, 1886.   F.C.C. BARRII.
A lovely pale yellow flower with crimson-edged
cup ; probably the most useful of all the Narcissi,
regard being had to its beauty, good constitution
and rapid increase.

Coronatus (*Krelage*).—April 14, 1885.   F.C.C. SELF-
YELLOW AJAX.   The finest of the *Spurius* group.
Light yellow perianth, broad and spreading ; well
expanded, full yellow trumpet.

Countess Grey (*Willmott*).—April 24, 1900.   F.C.C.
JOHNSTONI.   " *Empress* " × *Triandrus*.   White
perianth of the substance and quality of its
parent " *Empress* "; long sulphur trumpet.

Cresset (*Willmott*).—April 22, 1902. A.M. BURBIDGEI
(" *Princess Mary* " × *P. Poetarum*).   Symmetrical flower of good substance of medium
size.   Round white perianth ; widely expanded
crown of glowing orange-red.

Cyclamineus (*Barr*).—April 12, 1887.   F.C.C. SELF-
YELLOW AJAX.   Very distinct, early and dwarf.
Clear self-yellow.   Perianth very much reflexed,

long narrow cylindrical trumpet, elegantly serrated. Height six inches.

Cygnet (*Barr*).—April 22, 1902. A.M. BICOLOR AJAX. Very pale Bicolor with long trumpet.

Dante (*Engleheart*). April 7, 1896. F.C.C. POETI-CUS (*P. Ornatus* × *P. Poetarum*). Flowers fairly early. Well formed round broad-petalled perianth ; crown deeply suffused red.

Day Star (*Engleheart*).—May 7, 1901. A.M. BUR-BIDGEI.* Large flat-built flower. Perianth ivory ; shallow orange-flushed crown.

Diadem (*Engleheart*).—April 26, 1898. A.M. BARRII. Creamy-yellow perianth ; very shallow, broad yellow, crown, with sharply defined line of bright red.

Diana (*Engleheart*). April 24, 1900. A.M. (INCOMP. × WHITE AJAX.) Distinct, noble and refined flower. Perianth large, bold, and creamy-white ; flat crown of pale cowslip-yellow.

Dorothy Kingsmill (*Kingsmill*). — April 24, 1900. F.C.C. JOHNSTONI (Grandis × Triandrus Cala-thinus). Very fine both in form and colour.

Dorothy Wemyss (*Willmott*).—May 7, 1901. A.M. BARRII. A very valuable old variety now first officially recognised. Large flower. Perianth creamy-white ; cup margined orange-red. The latest and one of the most beautiful of the Barrii class.

Dr Laumonier (*Wilks*). — April 27, 1897. A.M. BIFLORUS.

Duchess of Westminster (*Barr*). — April 27, 1886. F.C.C. LEEDSII. Large white perianth ; the long canary cup, orange edged at first opening, passes off pure white.

Duke of Bedford (*Barr*).—April 18, 1899. A.M. BICOLOR AJAX. Very early. Very large flower of fine form. Perianth segments broad; trumpet large and of soft clear yellow.

Earl Grey (*Willmott*). — April 23, 1901. F.C.C. JOHNSTONI (*Triandrus* × *Emperor*). Perianth cream - white; the long vase - shaped crown of pale creamy-amber. Form and colour suggestive of "*Triandrus*," but size nearly that of "*Emperor*."

Elaine (*Willmott*).—May 7, 1901. F.C.C. LEEDSII. The whole flower pale ivory. Round perianth of fine substance; crown shallow and expanded.

Eleanor Berkeley (*Willmott*).—April 24, 1900. A.M. JOHNSTONI. Considered an improvement on "*Snowdrop*," with broader perianth and shorter and wider trumpet. Pure white.

Ellen Willmott (*Engleheart*).—March 23, 1897. F.C.C. BICOLOR AJAX. Massive Bicolor of very high quality. Perianth pure white, of remarkable substance; trumpet very bright yellow.

Flambeau (*Engleheart*).—April 18, 1899. A.M. IN-COMP. Yellow perianth and glowing orange-red crown. Intermediate in character and time of flowering between "*C. J. Backhouse*" and "*Gloria Mundi*."

Florence (*Engleheart*).—April 23, 1901. A.M. WHITE AJAX. Good size. Perianth ivory, twisted at points; trumpet ivory-maize.

Fred Moore (*Barr*).—April 27, 1897. A.M. YELLOW AJAX. Large flower of good substance. Large, broad, primrose perianth; very large deep-golden trumpet, wide at mouth.

George Engleheart (*Engleheart*). — April 22, 1890. A.M. Hybrid from Tazetta *Bazelman Major* × *Poeticus Ornatus*. Perianth white, cup pale yellow with bright yellow margin.

Gloria Mundi (*Barr*).—May 10, 1887. F.C.C. IN-

COMP. Exceedingly good flower. In good
seasons the dusky-red of the cup contrasts finely
with the rich clear yellow perianth. In bad
seasons, however, the red colouring comes too
pale and is at times altogether wanting.

Glory of Leiden (*Barr*). — May 10, 1887. F.C.C.
SELF-YELLOW AJAX. Is best described as a
huge "*Emperor*," but is more refined in form.
The fine trumpet is of deeper yellow than the
perianth. A splendid flower of great substance
when well grown and from a good stock.

Glory of Noordwyk (*Veitch*).—April 22, 1902. A.M.
YELLOW AJAX. Pale yellow perianth; full
yellow trumpet. Very large flower.

Golden Bell (*Engleheart*).—April 12, 1892. F.C.C.
YELLOW AJAX. Graceful drooping flower. Very
large deep yellow trumpet with widely expanded
brim; broad perianth segments of pale yellow
and somewhat twisted.

Henry Irving (*Ware*).—April 27, 1886. F.C.C. SELF-
YELLOW AJAX. Large, clear, self-yellow of the
Spurius class, with wheel-like perianth. One of
the very earliest.

Herrick (*Engleheart*).—April 23, 1901. A.M. POETI-
CUS (*P. Ornatus* × *P. Poetarum*). Substantial
segments; deep red crown.

Hesperus (*Engleheart*).—May 2, 1899. A.M. BARRII.
Perianth creamy-buff, with deep apricot-orange
crown.

Hodsock's Pride (*Mellish*)—April 10, 1894. A.M.
BICOLOR AJAX. Huge in size, and suggestive of
"*Princeps*" in character.

Homer (*Engleheart*).—April 12, 1898. F.C.C. POETI-
CUS. Very large Ornatus-like perianth; crown
orange with a very broad band of clear deep
crimson. A very fine flower.

Hybrids (*Engleheart*).—March 22, 1892. B.C.

Hybrids between Poeticus and Biflorus (*Laumonier*).—
April 19, 1892. B.C. Flowers similar to
"Biflorus," but perianth slightly larger and
whiter, and cup distinctly margined with orange.
Interesting because Biflorus had hitherto been
considered absolutely sterile.

Incognita (*Willmott*).—April 22, 1902. A.M. BUR-
BIDGEI.* Flat-crowned class. Good white perianth; short well-expanded crown of "Queen
Sophia" colour, a beautiful and peculiar shade of
orange-apricot.

Ivanhoe (*Veitch*).—April 26, 1898. A.M. NELSONI.
Small neat flower. Perianth clear white; crown
orange.

James Dickson (*Dickson*).—April 8, 1884. F.C.C.
INCOMP.

J. B. M. Camm (*Barr*).—April 8, 1884. F.C.C.
BICOLOR AJAX. Very attractive flower. Symmetrical white perianth; trumpet much frilled, of
a soft lemon shade passing off nearly white.

Johnstoni [type] (*Barr*).—April 26, 1884. F.C.C.
Beautiful clear shade of lemon-yellow. *N. Ajax*
× *N. Triandrus.*

Juncifolius (*Backhouse*).—May 2, 1865. F.C.C. Slender
growing, dwarf species, rush-leaved. The smallest
Narcissus; height three to four inches. Rich
yellow colour, with perfectly flat crown.

King Alfred (*Kendall*).—March 22, 1899. F.C.C.
SELF-YELLOW AJAX. Probably the finest yellow
Ajax yet produced. Very tall, large flower of
uniform rich golden colour and of great substance. Said to be a cross between *Maximus* and
either *Emperor* or *Golden Spur*. Very graceful
perianth; trumpet large, elegant, with open,
deeply-frilled mouth.

Lady Helen Vincent (*Barr*).—April 12, 1898. A.M.
SELF-YELLOW AJAX. A large, refined flower of
uniform soft, clear yellow. Somewhat after the
style of Glory of Leiden.

Lady Margaret Boscawen (*Engleheart*).—April 2, 1898.
F.C.C. INCOMP. *Horsfieldi* × *P. Ornatus.* A large
and beautiful flower of the "Sir Watkin" class,
but with its remarkably broad, flat segments of
clear white.

Lettice Harmer (*Engleheart*).—March 23, 1897. A.M.
BICOLOR AJAX. Yellow trumpet, in form somewhat resembling that of Mad. de Graaff; white,
much overlapping perianth segments.

Lord Roberts (*Barr*).—April 23, 1901. F.C.C. SELF-
YELLOW AJAX. A very large, massive and
symmetrical flower of the "Emperor" class.
Full yellow.

Lucifer (*Engleheart*).—April 12, 1898. A.M.; April
23, 1901. F.C.C. INCOMP. Large white perianth,
with large, glowing red, tubular crown. There
is an inferior variety "*Vesuvius*," which is sometimes mistaken for true "*Lucifer*."

Lulworth (*Engleheart*).—April 10, 1894. F.C.C.
INCOMP. A flower of exquisite beauty, said to
be a chance seedling found in an orchard at
Lulworth. Perianth segments broad, ample and
slightly drooping; at first very pale sulphur, but
afterwards pure white; cup large, bell-shaped,
and of a peculiarly vivid red.

Madame de Graaff (*Barr*).—May 10, 1887. F.C.C.
WHITE AJAX. One of the largest, finest, and
most distinct of the white daffodils; has substance and constitution as strong as a *Bicolor*.
The trumpet, which is elegantly rolled back at
the brim, is pale lemon at first, and changes after
a few days to a beautiful waxy white.

Maggie May (*Engleheart*).—April 18, 1899.   F.C.C.
LEEDSII.   Flower of great size with fine frilled
cup of pale citron colour.   The white perianth
segments have a rather drooping, some think a
too drooping, habit.

Marina (*Engleheart*).—May 2, 1899.   A.M.   INCOMP.
White spreading creamy perianth, with large,
shallow open crown of pale lemon.

Master at Arms (*Engleheart*).—April 23, 1901.   A.M.
INCOMP.   A stoutly-built bicolor Incomparabilis
with short, broad crown.

Minnie (*Van Waveren*).—April 24, 1900.   A.M.
INCOMP. or NELSONI.   Fine flower.   Perianth
white; cup yellow.

Monophyllus (*Ware*).—December 7, 1886.   F.C.C.
CORBULARIA.   The exquisite, snowy white,
winter - flowering Hoop - petticoat Daffodil of
Algeria.   Too delicate for ordinary cultivation.

Moonbeam (*R. O. Backhouse*).—May 7, 1901.   F.C.C.
LEEDSII.   Firm, flat, circular perianth, and short
white cup; a perfect flower.

Moon-ray (*Willmott*).—May 6, 1902.   A.M.   JOHN-
STONI.   A very elegant drooping flower.

Mrs Berkeley (*Willmott*).—April 24, 1900.   F.C.C.
TRIANDRUS × MINNIE HUME.   A nearly white
"*Sir Watkin.*"   Perianth pure white and of great
substance.   Crown passing nearly white.   Has
longer pedicel and paler colour than "*Robert
Berkeley.*"   Most beautiful.

Mrs (J. B. M.) Camm (*Barr*).—May 8, 1888.   F.C.C.
WHITE AJAX.   Perianth white and elegant;
trumpet pale primrose passing to white.   This
and "*Mrs Vincent*" are, when well grown,
probably the most elegant of the white daffodils.

Naiad (*Engleheart*).—April 27, 1897.   F.C.C.   N.
POETICUS × TRIANDRUS.   Clear white flowers

with pale straw-coloured cup; the flowers produced three and four in the bunch.

Olympia (*Van Waveren*).—April 24, 1900. A.M. YELLOW AJAX. A fine large flower.

Oriflamme (*Engleheart*).—April 12, 1898. A.M. BUR-BIDGEI. White perianth of fine circular form, with entire cup of fiery red.

Pallidus præcox (*Barr*).—February 12, 1884. F.C.C. SULPHUR AJAX. Variable in size and shade from pale straw-colour to white. Very early. Very delicate in constitution. Does best in grass.

Peter Barr (*Barr*).—April 8, 1902. F.C.C. WHITE AJAX. Huge flower, cream-coloured self, with fine trumpet. A noble flower.

Petrarch (*Engleheart*).—April 7, 1896. A.M. POETI-CUS. (*P. Ornatus* × *P. Recurvus.*)

Philip Hurt (*Engleheart*).—May 5, 1896. A.M. BER-NARDI. Originally introduced by Rev. Wolley Dod. The finest of the Bernardi class. Perianth white; cup brilliantly stained with very bright red.

Pope's King (*Pope*).—April 18, 1899. A.M. SELF-YELLOW AJAX. One of the early flowering Daffodils. Something after the style of *Golden Spur*, but larger and with a distinct greeny-tinge in the perianth segments.

Primrose Phœnix (*Walker*).—April 22, 1902. A.M. DOUBLE INCOMP. A very fine fully double flower of a soft primrose shade.

Princess Mary (*Barr*).—April 8, 1884. F.C.C. INCOMP. A most refined and distinct flower, with broad creamy perianth segments, and orange-stained widely expanded cup.

Queen Alexandra (*Kendall*).—April 22, 1902. A.M. INCOMP. A fine large flower. White perianth; vivid red cup.

Queen Christina (*Barr*).—April 22, 1902. A.M. BICOLOR AJAX. Colouring of " Ellen Willmott." Trumpet open at mouth and frilled. A large fine flower.

Queen Emma (*Veitch*).—April 12, 1902. A.M. SELF-YELLOW AJAX. A large Dutch Ajax.

Queen of England (*Barr*).—April 8, 1884. F.C.C. LEEDSII. Large white perianth; large expanded canary cup, after the style of " Minnie Hume."

Queen Sophia (*Barr*).—April 8, 1884. F.C.C. INCOMP. A remarkable and beautiful flower. Perianth sulphur, large spreading frilled cup of a peculiar bright orange-apricot shade.

Queen Wilhelmina. (See "*Wilhelmina*.")

Rear Guard (*Engleheart*).—May 7, 1901. A.M. NELSONI. Large, late, solid-flowered. Hybrid of " Grandis." Firm, flat-set, overlapping segments of ivory-white; cylindrical crown of rich yellow.

Rupicola (*Elwes*).—April 4, 1887. Highly commended. Sub-species of JUNCIFOLIUS.

Revd. C. Wolley Dod (*Willmott*).—April 24, 1900. A.M. JOHNSTONI. Large bicolor more inclined to the form of *Incomparabilis* than any other hybrid of *Ajax* and *Triandrus*.

Robert Berkeley (*Willmott*).—April 23, 1901. F.C.C. TRIANDRUS × MINNIE HUME. After the style of *Mrs Berkeley*, but sturdier and not so pale in colour of crown.

Sea Bird (*Engleheart*).—May 7, 1901. A.M. INCOMP. Of very large size. The ample white segments are undulated; the cup deep and of pure yellow with darker edge. Pale green tones at base of segments and very noticeable dark-green eye.

Sir Francis Drake (*Kendall*).—April 8, 1902. A.M.

MAGNI-CORONATI
(*A Pseudo-Narcissus form*)
BICOLOR AJAX "QUEEN CHRISTINA"

SELF-YELLOW AJAX. Resembles a huge " *Emperor.*" Not so deep a yellow as " *King Alfred,*" and without the marked *Maximus* character.

Snowdrop (*Engleheart*).—April 13, 1897. F.C.C. JOHNSTONI. (*N. Cernuus* × *N. Triandrus.*) Very beautiful, pure white and elegantly drooping flower. Large and most refined. With horizontal spreading perianth, and long tubular trumpet.

Southern Star (*Engleheart*).—March 23, 1897. F.C.C. BURBIDGEI. Broad, stout, white perianth segments. Cup wide and spreading, with broad rich orange-red border.

Spenser (*Engleheart*).—May 7, 1901. A.M. POETICUS. Of great solidity. Broad red crown. Cross between *P. Poetarum* and *P. Recurvus* ; and intermediate in season.

St Cecilia (*Engleheart*).—April 23, 1901. A.M. WHITE AJAX. A refined flower with segments broad and spreading; trumpet long and well opened, ivory in colour, with a pink tone inside.

Stella Superba (*Walter Ware*).—April 23, 1901. A.M. INCOMP. A great improvement on the old variety " *Stella,*"¸of which it is almost double the size. Long white spreading perianth segments ; clear yellow cup.

Strongbow (*Engleheart*).—April 18, 1899. A.M. NELSONI. A flower of good substance. The white segments are broad and flat, the rich yellow crown much expanded.

Sunset (*Barr*).—April 18, 1899. A.M. INTERMEDIUS. Said to be a hybrid between *Tazetta* and *Jonquilla.* Yellow perianth ; orange-red cup, which in good seasons is very fine ; clustered.

Tazetta flore pleno (*Veitch*). — March 18, 1874. F.C.C.

Torch (*Engleheart*).—April 8, 1902.   A.M.   Incomp.   A huge flower with exceedingly fine,
large, vividly red cup.   Had the yellow perianth
segments been equally good it would have ranked
as a splendidly first-class flower; but though
rather weak in the perianth it is a very showy
and decorative *border* plant.   Early.

Trimon (*Barr*).—February 14, 1899.   A.M.   N.
Triandrus × N. Monophyllus.   The small
milk-white flowers are intermediate between its
parents.

Van Waveren's Giant (*Van Waveren*).—April 24, 1900.
F.C.C.   Yellow Ajax.   A huge flower.

Victoria (*Barr*).—April 27, 1897.   A.M.   Bicolor
Ajax.   Broad creamy white perianth; trumpet
rich yellow, large, flanged and frilled.   Particularly good when grown under glass.

Virgil (*Engleheart*).—April 24, 1900.   A.M.   Poeticus.   A very good flower.   One of the new
Poeticus section.

Warley Magna (*Willmott*).—April 22, 1902.   A.M.
White Ajax.   A large and very beautiful flower.

Watchfire (*Willmott*).—May 6, 1902.   A.M.   Burbidgei.*   Fine   white   perianth.   Splendid
orange-red crown.   Late flowering.

Weardale Perfection (*Barr*).—April 10, 1894.   F.C.C.
Bicolor Ajax.   One of the largest and tallest
Daffodils.   Beautiful in colouring, the solid
perianth segments being white and the immense
trumpet of a very pale primrose colour.

White Lady (*Engleheart*).—April 20, 1898.   A.M.
Leedsii.   Broad white perianth of fine form;
elegantly frilled cup of pale canary yellow.   An
improved "Katherine Spurrell."

White Muticus (*Revd. C. Digby*).—April 22, 1902.
B.C.   Very beautiful and distinct.

White Queen (*Engleheart*).—April 12, 1898. F.C.C. LEEDSII. One of the very finest Narcissi. In the way of "Sir Watkin," but having the broad perianth of glistening white, and the very large cup of pale citron passing to white.

White Wings (*Engleheart*).—April 26, 1898. A.M. NELSONI. Somewhat in the way of "*Nelsoni pulchellus*," but larger and every way superior. Very shapely round white perianth; expanded crown of clear yellow.

Wilhelmina (*J. de Groot*).—April 24, 1900. A.M. BICOLOR AJAX. A fine large Dutch flower; two shades of pale creamy-yellow.

Will Scarlett (*Engleheart*).—April 26, 1898. F.C.C. INCOMP. A remarkable flower with white perianth, and very large, widely expanded cup of exceeding brilliant orange-scarlet.

But there are a great many flowers of eminent beauty which have not yet been certificated. This for several reasons. Some have not been presented to the Committee. Some splendid varieties have been necessarily presented when the flowers were either too young or too old, and so could not be judged at their best. Some, though most excellent, have not been thought sufficiently distinct from other flowers which had previously made a name for themselves. We are, therefore, not surprised to find many first-class flowers that are not in the above list.

The following are some new varieties of very great excellence which have come under the notice of the present writer, and which he believes will, though not certificated, be among the prominent flowers of the good collections of the future.

List of exceptionally fine varieties not yet certificated.

Almira.—POETICUS. Excellent. Of *Ornatus* character
and fine substance.

Ariadne.—LEEDSII.   A great improvement in every
way on the old variety Leedsii "*Princess of
Wales*," with good white perianth and very fine
expanded pale lemon cup.

Astrardente.—BURBIDGEI.*   Very distinct.   Much
expanded flat crown of beautiful salmon shade.
This belongs to a new, distinct, and very attractive type of *Burbidgei*, which Mr Engleheart has
produced in his most successful cross-fertilising
labours.   The crown takes the form of a disc,
very wide (relatively), but having no depth to
speak of.   After the same style are "Egret"
and "Imogen" [see below], which make excellent
companion flowers to it, and several others.

Blood Orange.—BURBIDGEI.*   Large flower; pale
lemon segments and very fine deep-scarlet
crown.

Bridal Flower.—LEEDSII.   (*Albicans* × *P. Ornatus.*)
Very telling white flower.

Bullfinch.—BURBIDGEI. Symmetrical flower with overlapping lemon segments fading to white; crown
heavily edged orange scarlet.

Celia.—BICOLOR AJAX. Excellent flower. Fine lemon
trumpet passing to white.

Chaucer.—POETICUS. One of the earliest of the new
Poeticus section, with circular *Ornatus*-shaped
perianth and large flat cup of bright scarlet.

Coronet.—BICOLOR AJAX. Improvement on "*Mrs
Walter Ware*," and distinguished by its dark
golden-yellow trumpet.

Egret—BURBIDGEI. Broad solid white perianth, much

expanded disc-like crown of lemon darkened by beautiful gold margin and shading.

Electra.—INCOMP. A very beautiful flower of two shades of yellow.

Enid.—LEEDSII. Very tall and robust. Perianth segments ivory-white, broad and long; long cup-shaped crown of cream colour.

Epic.—POETICUS. One of the very finest of the new *Poeticus* section. Solid flowers of great size; crown brilliant red. Early.

Firebrand.—INCOMP. White perianth; long cup of very deep and glowing red.

Flamingo.—INCOMP. Long and prettily shaped pale yellow segments. Fine red cup. (The stalk is inclined to be weak.)

Genoa.—WHITE AJAX. A very fine white flower.

Glory.—POETICUS. An early and very fine form of the new *Poeticus* section.

Herald.—SELF-YELLOW AJAX. A distinct improvement on "Emperor"; said to flower side by side with it about seven days earlier.

Horace.—POETICUS. Thought by some to be the best of the new *Poeticus* section. Overlapping rounded perianth segments, with flat and entirely scarlet crown.

Imogen.—BURBIDGEI. Much expanded flat disc-like crown of pale orange-yellow. Must not be confounded with the now obsolete *Barrii* "Imogen."

Jeannie Woodhouse.—BICOLOR AJAX. Very pretty, rather small flower.

Lady Watkin.—INCOMP. A small and better shaped "Sir Watkin," with cup strongly suffused orange.

Laura.—POETICUS. Early. An improved *Poeticus Ornatus*.

Laureate.—POETICUS. A very fine flower of the new *Poeticus* section.

Lilian.—Leedsii. (*White Ajax* × *P. Ornatus.*) Fine white perianth with broad, well-formed segments; long cup of beautiful shade of pale lemon.

Monarch.—Yellow Ajax. A very fine flower of refined form, good substance and large size; full yellow.

Mrs Morland Crosfield.—Bicolor Ajax. A large fine flower; large perianth pure white; long well shaped clear yellow trumpet.

Norma.—Bicolor Ajax. Very fine. Elegant trumpet of paler yellow than the ordinary bicolor type.

Occident.—Burbidgei.* An improved "*Baroness Heath.*"

Ptarmigan.—Incomp. Perianth pure white and overlapping, with expanded lemon cup.

Sea Gull.—Probably Burbidgei. A beautiful companion flower to *Albatross* (and from the same seed pod). It differs in having a *very much* paler rim of orange colour in the crown.

Sceptre.—Burbidgei. Large flower. Perianth delicate primrose, fluted cup of bright fiery orange-red.

Solfatare.—Incomp. Large flat, broad segments, long widely expanded crown, the whole flower being of a uniform delicate lemon-yellow. Very distinct.

Warden.—Incomp. White perianth, yellow cup, elegant form. Remarkable for its good and substantial perianth segments.

Water-witch.—Leedsii. Long gracefully drooping white perianth segments; elegant white cup. An improved *Leedsii* "*Elegans.*"

CHAPTER XIV.

It is much easier to exhibit Daffodils nowadays than it was a few years ago. The leading show committees have begun to set fixed limits, not only to the number of varieties to be shown in each "collection," but also to the number of blooms in each vase of any exhibit. The characteristic beauties of the different varieties are quite as well displayed by five or six blooms artistically arranged as by the large jars of unlimited numbers which used to be set up. This is a great gain to exhibitors. It much reduces the amount of luggage to be transported, and it saves those who with comparatively few bulbs have fine varieties and well-grown flowers from being overwhelmed by the mass of possibly inferior flowers which larger but less careful growers may set up against them.

There are now plenty of shows at which to exhibit. Numerous silver cups, medals, and other valuable prizes are annually offered at convenient centres—*e.g.* at the Drill Hall, Westminster (R.H.S. Show), the great Birmingham Show of the Midland Daffodil Society, the Truro Show of the Cornwall Daffodil Society, at Edinburgh, Dublin, Manchester, Ipswich, Norwich, Wisbeach, and many other places in different parts of the country. Suitable vases for staging the flowers are usually provided by the show committees; and at many of these shows, notably at Birmingham and Truro, the staging arrangements are remarkably good, and the convenience of the exhibitors most carefully studied.

A little forethought at planting time will much improve the chances of the intending exhibitor. It is very annoying to find as the show day approaches that some of the varieties which have been relied upon for effect are either too far past or not forward enough for staging. This contingency may be partly guarded against in the case of any particularly useful varieties by planting two or three patches with different aspects and surroundings, so as to ensure a longer succession of flowers. Bulbs planted rather more deeply than usual, in heavier soil, and with a northerly aspect, will produce a later batch of flowers than those planted at the usual depth, in light soil and in a warm situation. The flowering of the bulbs may be farther retarded by late planting, but it should be always remembered that late-planted bulbs cannot be expected to produce such fine flowers as those planted at the proper time. It is also advisable, if it can be managed, to grow in cold frames some boxes of the showiest and best of the later-flowering varieties. These flowers will, with proper management, be quite as good or better than those in the open border, and about ten days earlier, and will be very useful on the show table.

As the show day approaches, it will be wise of the exhibitor to take stock of the varieties which seem likely to be in flower at the right time, and to make a rough *general* plan of the relative positions in which they will look best when staged. Flowers with a slightly drooping habit, which consequently show best when looked at from below—such as the beautiful Leedsii *Katherine Spurrell*, Barrii *Maurice Vilmorin*, and many other Incomparables—should be reserved for the highest shelf of the staging. Most of the short-stalked flowers, and almost all the Trumpets, look well in the lower rows, while the smaller white Trumpets are very effective on the bottom row of all. The best and most striking varieties should be massed, as far as possible, in the

centre of the exhibit, as this gives dignity and brings
out the strength of the collection. Again, it is of great
importance to arrange the different kinds so that their
colouring and other characteristics may mutually set
each other off to the best advantage. Thus the red-
cupped varieties should be judiciously distributed among
the whites and yellows and bicolors, to bring out the
beauty of the more quietly coloured flowers. Such
telling flowers as Incomparabilis *Mary Anderson* and
Queen Sophia will lose in beauty if placed side by side,
and will appear poor and ineffective if put near such
a flower as *Lulworth*, with its cup of unusually vivid
red. A good and varied collection of Narcissi when
well arranged will give a beautiful symphony of colour,
and it is better not to leave this arrangement to be
settled amid the harassing bustle of the exhibition hall
at staging time.

A rough outline as to the arrangement of the flowers
having been formed, the next anxiety will be to secure
as many varieties as possible for staging; and careful
preparation will often increase the exhibitor's choice of
varieties by twenty per cent. A fortnight before the
show day he should begin to collect any specially large
buds which are ready to cut, and keep them in a darkened room made as cool and airy as possible. Lumps of
charcoal should be put in the water, which should be
changed when necessary. At intervals of several days,
very thin slices may be cut off from the ends of the
flower-stalks; this will prolong their life a day or two.
Flowers of *Maximus*, and many large-growing kinds,
when thus treated, often continue fit for exhibition a
fortnight after cutting, and *Johnstoni Queen of Spain* even
longer. On the other hand, buds which are coming on
too slowly may be cut a little prematurely and coaxed
out in water, in a very warm temperature, a day or two
sooner than in the natural course, with little or no loss

of beauty and character. But the best flowers for exhibition are generally those which are cut as the bud begins to break, about five or six days before the show day, and allowed to open in a moderately warm room.

Every exhibitor should make a point of showing his flowers clean and fresh and in the finest condition possible. To this end he should always gather them before the bud quite unfolds itself and open them under cover, uninjured by wind, dust, sun and rain. Then again, very careful packing for their journey is of supreme importance. A good plan is to pack in shallow boxes, each box just taking one layer of flowers, arranged in rows so that they mutually support each other, with a little dry tissue paper used to fill up empty spaces and keep everything in place. It is a great mistake to pack Daffodils for a journey in damp cotton wool.

Of course additional flowers should always be taken, over and above those actually required for staging ; and all should be unpacked and revived in water several hours before they come under the judge's eye.

In the matter of staging the following additional hints may be useful.

Now that bulbs of so many very excellent varieties may be obtained at a moderate cost, none of those which are poor in form or colour should be staged, unless it should be absolutely necessary to do so in order to make up the required number in the exhibit ; but it is better to show fine, well-grown flowers of really good ordinary kinds, than flowers of expensive and scarce varieties in poor or doubtful condition.

The exhibit should be made as widely representative as possible. Most judges, other things being about equal, will give first place to the exhibit which shows the greatest variety of form and colour, and which is best representative of the different sections.

Daffodil flowers always look best when set up with

HOW NOT TO EXHIBIT DAFFODILS

Note that the three centre flowers are well arranged, but the four at the sides should be turned more to the front, and the whole group should be more compact without being stiff.

Daffodil leaves. A supply of these should be secured from clumps of the common double or other strong-growing inexpensive varieties.

A little damp moss should be used for keeping the flowers in the desired position in the vases, and they should be tastefully arranged with their faces turned, some wholly, some partly, to the front, and so that all may catch the eye. The judges ought to be able to see the full beauty of the exhibit at once, without any moving of the flowers or vases.

In the event of vases not being provided for exhibitors at any Daffodil show, the flowers look very well staged in small-sized ordinary brown blacking bottles, which when properly cleaned have an excellent appearance, and being very strong are easily packed for travelling.

Such are a few of the secrets of success in exhibiting Daffodils. Over and above these the golden rule must be followed—*Do everything carefully.* Then it ought not to be difficult for an enthusiastic grower who has well-selected varieties to secure a medal or even a cup, in evidence of his skilful cultivation.

INDEX.

Black-faced type (thus **N. Pseudo-Narcissus**) denotes a species.
Italic capitals (thus *N. BARRII*) denote a typical hybrid.
Small capitals (thus N. Muticus) denote a sub-species, or a variety of marked importance.
Italic type (thus *N. Albicans*) denotes a form of less marked importance, and double forms.
Garden hybrids and seedlings (except those which are of old standing, or typical of groups) are printed in ordinary Roman type.

CPSIA information can be obtained at www.ICGtesting.com
Printed in the USA
LVOW10s2040190614

390831LV00030B/1129/P